MW00447959

PLANET

ENTREPRENEUR

PLANET

ENTREPRENEUR

**THE WORLD ENTREPRENEURSHIP FORUM'S GUIDE
TO BUSINESS SUCCESS AROUND THE WORLD**

STEVEN D. STRAUSS

AND MEMBERS OF THE WORLD ENTREPRENEURSHIP FORUM

WILEY

Cover image: World Flags © iStockphoto.com/mstay
Cover design: Wiley

Copyright © 2014 by Steven D. Strauss. All rights reserved.

Published by John Wiley & Sons, Inc., Hoboken, New Jersey.
Published simultaneously in Canada.

No part of this publication may be reproduced, stored in a retrieval system, or transmitted in any form or by any means, electronic, mechanical, photocopying, recording, scanning, or otherwise, except as permitted under Section 107 or 108 of the 1976 United States Copyright Act, without either the prior written permission of the Publisher, or authorization through payment of the appropriate per-copy fee to the Copyright Clearance Center, 222 Rosewood Drive, Danvers, MA 01923, (978) 750–8400, fax (978) 646–8600, or on the web at www.copyright.com. Requests to the Publisher for permission should be addressed to the Permissions Department, John Wiley & Sons, Inc., 111 River Street, Hoboken, NJ 07030, (201) 748–6011, fax (201) 748–6008, or online at www.wiley.com/go/permissions.

Limit of Liability/Disclaimer of Warranty: While the publisher and author have used their best efforts in preparing this book, they make no representations or warranties with the respect to the accuracy or completeness of the contents of this book and specifically disclaim any implied warranties of merchantability or fitness for a particular purpose. No warranty may be created or extended by sales representatives or written sales materials. The advice and strategies contained herein may not be suitable for your situation. You should consult with a professional where appropriate. Neither the publisher nor the author shall be liable for damages arising herefrom.

For general information about our other products and services, please contact our Customer Care Department within the United States at (800) 762–2974, outside the United States at (317) 572–3993 or fax (317) 572–4002.

Wiley publishes in a variety of print and electronic formats and by print-on-demand. Some material included with standard print versions of this book may not be included in e-books or in print-on-demand. If this book refers to media such as a CD or DVD that is not included in the version you purchased, you may download this material at http://booksupport.wiley.com. For more information about Wiley products, visit www.wiley.com.

Library of Congress Cataloging-in-Publication Data:
Planet entrepreneur : the World Entrepreneurship Forum's guide to business success around the world / [edited by] Steven D. Strauss.
  pages cm
  Includes index.
  ISBN 978-1-118-78952-0 (cloth); ISBN 978-1-118-81075-0 (ebk);
ISBN 978-1-118-81099-6 (ebk)
  1. Entrepreneurship. 2. Success in business. I. Strauss, Steven D., 1958-
II. World Entrepreneurship Forum.
  HB615.P52 2014
  658.4'21–dc23

2013028889

Printed in the United States of America

10 9 8 7 6 5 4 3 2 1

CONTENTS

ABOUT THE WORLD ENTREPRENEURSHIP FORUM

The World Entrepreneurship Forum is a unique concept. It embraces the totality of the entrepreneurial ecosystem, including business entrepreneurs, social entrepreneurs, policy makers, experts, and academics.

It is a community of entrepreneurship from five continents and a powerful global network of leaders selected for their achievements and commitment to society. Every year, the Forum gathers over 250 participants, coming from 60 countries, willing to join with their peers to think, act, and transform their environment.

It is both a think tank and a do tank:

- Members share the latest trends and issues about global entrepreneurship.
- They develop ideas and recommendations aimed at promoting and spreading entrepreneurship worldwide.
- They facilitate entrepreneurial initiatives on a local or global scale.

The World Entrepreneurship Forum promotes the development of entrepreneurship, creating wealth and social justice. This dual approach, economic and social, is one of the distinguishing features of the Forum.

The Forum's "Entrepreneur for the World" Awards showcases internationally renowned role models who illustrate the Forum's core values of entrepreneurship that creates wealth and social justice, in the following five categories:

1. Entrepreneur
2. Young entrepreneur
3. Social entrepreneur

4. Educational entrepreneur
5. Policy maker

The Junior World Entrepreneurship Forums (two- and three-day forums in universities) are meant to give voice to junior entrepreneurial causes and initiatives worldwide.

The World Entrepreneurship Forum also develops local events and initiatives, to be hosted within local, regional, or national chapters and emphasizing the dynamism, the networks, the best practices, and the entrepreneurial challenges of the country.

Since 2008, the World Entrepreneurship Forum has seen 600 participants, 75 countries, 4 white papers, 50 listed best practices, 18 rewarded role models, 10,000 students attending Junior Forums in 18 countries, 150 press articles in 35 countries in 2012, 1 online collaborative platform, and 5 founding partners from Europe and Asia.

www.world-entrepreneurship-forum.com
contact@world-entrepreneurship-forum.com

WORLD ENTREPRENEURSHIP FORUM'S FOUNDING MEMBERS DEFINITION

EMLYON Business School

Founded in 1872, affiliated with the Chamber of Commerce and Industry of Lyon, EMLYON Business School is one of the major European business schools. It is devoted to lifelong learning for entrepreneurial and international management. Its pedagogy is focused on educating entrepreneurs for the world. (See www.em-lyon.com.)

KPMG

KPMG is a global network of professional services firms providing audit, tax, and advisory services to a wide variety of public and private sector organizations in 156 countries.

We act as responsible corporate citizens and are committed to our communities and environments. KPMG France therefore decided back in 2008 to co-found the World Entrepreneurship Forum with EMLYON Business School, acknowledging the tremendous role and importance of entrepreneurship in enabling economic growth, wealth, employment, and social justice throughout the world.

ACE

The Action Community for Entrepreneurship (ACE) is a Singaporean movement for entrepreneurs, by entrepreneurs. ACE helps aspiring entrepreneurs start up by building a vibrant community and connecting them to resources, people, and knowledge. ACE is currently led by

Mr. Teo Ser Luck, Singapore Minister of State for Trade and Industry. Please visit us at www.ace.sg.

Nanyang Technological University

A research-intensive public university, Nanyang Technological University (NTU) has 33,500 undergraduate and postgraduate students in the colleges of Engineering, Business, Science, Humanities, Arts, and Social Sciences (and Medicine in 2013). A fast-growing university with an international outlook, NTU is putting its global stamp on Five Peaks of Excellence: Sustainable Earth, Future Healthcare, New Media, New Silk Road, and Innovation Asia. For more information, please visit www.ntu.edu.sg.

ONLYLYON

ONLYLYON is in charge of promoting Lyon's assets and bringing its ambition to fruition: turning its economic development model into a reference among other major European cities and establishing its international influence. It has been created by Lyon's main partners and economic institutions, among them Greater Lyon Council and Lyon's Chamber of Commerce and Industry. (See www.onlylyon.org.)

Zhejiang University

One of China's oldest institutions of higher education, Zhejiang University is a leading national comprehensive and research university with the motto of "Faith of Truth." Its School of Management is known for the research and business education, especially in entrepreneurship and innovation, and it is the first state-run business school in mainland China that has received international accreditation. (See www.zju.edu.cn.)

PREFACE

The World Entrepreneurship Forum, the first think tank fully dedicated to entrepreneurship, was created six years ago based on the idea that, more than ever, the world would need entrepreneurs of any kind in the coming decades. Six years have passed, and the current worldwide crisis and increasing unpredictability of events show that the original idea proves to be very relevant. In fact, throughout the world, entrepreneurship is on the way to becoming the dominant business philosophy, since it combines virtues such as creativity, innovation, initiative, and flexibility and, above all, is at the basis of job creation. At the same time, the spirit of entrepreneurship is expanding dramatically to the social area. Modern-day social entrepreneurs are using business models to develop social ventures at the bottom of the pyramid. The Nobel Peace Prize awarded to Muhammad Yunus and Grameen Bank in 2006 illustrated the global scale of the phenomenon.

Our conviction is that the increasing interest of policy makers and public opinion for entrepreneurs both in emerging and developed countries is related to the urgent need to find solutions to the new challenges and mega trends that require a new paradigm. Old models are not able to bring answers to current issues. Yesterday's institutions, business models, and social systems are no longer operating. Hence, the entrepreneurial spirit has to be extended to all areas to invent not only new products, services, and business models but also new institutions of regulations and new social models (above and beyond).

Jeremy Rifkin thinks that the Third Industrial Revolution (2011) will be driven by the convergence of Internet communication and renewable energies. According to him, big revolutionary transformations take place when there is a convergence between new communication means/infrastructure technologies and a new energy era. Current opportunities of transformations created by the convergence of digital technologies, nanotechnologies, biotechnologies, and neurosciences combining with the need of inventing a new "energy regime" are definitely giving rise to an industrial revolution. However, we believe that discontinuities and transformations are broader and more dramatic than merely an industrial revolution. Indeed, four major transformations (demographic, geopolitical, technological, and environmental) have been converging or diverging, and the world has been entering in the era of the most important discontinuities a human being has ever experienced since the first Industrial Revolution.

Population growth, from 7 billion in 2010 to 9 billion in 2050, raises the challenge of getting billions of people out of poverty. Maybe more importantly, for the first time in human history, life expectancy will be close to a century by 2050, raising another challenge, which is inventing new institutions and new social life adapted to a world that will gather four generations instead of three.

Within the same time span, the gravity center of the world economy will shift from developed Western countries to emerging big demographic blocs. That will give place to a new global geopolitical order. China, India, Brazil, Russia, the United States, and Europe as global superpowers and Mexico, Indonesia, Turkey, and South Africa as regional powers will interact and compete in order to define new rules of the economic and political game. As Hubert Védrine, French Foreign Minister in 1997–2002, said in his recent book in 2012, "for the first time in history there is such a competition between so many powers." Indeed, the multipolar global world is not about homogenization by the expansion of Western 'universal' values. But it is rather a high level of interconnections and interactions between different institutional systems and economic ethos that are in competition. Every day, we learn that modernization is not unique but multiple. Different kinds of modernity rooted in different economic and social ethos are in competition.

The current trend of decoupling between high-growth countries and developed economies may lead us toward 2050 with a new economic order in which two thirds of world GNP will be set up by the current eight major emerging countries. It means that several billion people will reach the living standards of the less than one billion people from the

Westernized world. That is to say that a huge middle class will coexist likely with a large number of poor people excluded by the development of the global economy.

Rising expectations of the new middle class of the emerging world are indeed very legitimate. As the big demographic blocs of the emerging world catch up, that is good news from the perspective of the equity. But could it be believed that this good news is sustainable under the current mode of production which is largely dependent upon non-renewable resources?

Systematic degradation of the global climate and depletion of natural resources under the regime of carbon-based energy and modes of production depending on intensive use of nonrenewable resources create contradiction with positive megatrends. Combined with the population growth and the high growth of the emerging countries, this degradation puts high pressure even on very basic and vital resources such as water and air.

Hence, the question is the following: How can we use the potential of positive convergence and at the same time solve the problem raised by the divergence in the transformations? To put it in different words: How can we invent sustainable growth with the global citizenship spirit? It is more than the Industrial Revolution; it is about inventing New Humanism.

Entrepreneurs are central agents for turning all of these challenges and discontinuities into solutions and disruptive changes by inventing new business models, social patterns, and new institutions.

The aim of the World Entrepreneurship Forum is to contribute to shape this new humanism by putting together business entrepreneurs, social entrepreneurs, policy makers, and other leaders involved into a global entrepreneurship ecosystem sharing the same value and belief: Entrepreneurs are creators of the wealth and borderless social justice.

In a multipolar world where three main economic ethos—liberal economic ethos, coordinated market economic ethos, and informal economic ethos—are competing, it is very important, also, to bring any entrepreneurs coming from these main economic ethos to create inspiration through entrepreneurial stories, to set up recommendations to shape the New Humanism, and to take initiative to move toward the world of 2050.

This book presents the insights of 14 entrepreneurs who are part of the World Entrepreneurship Forum, coming from three different economic ethos. They are trying to change the world and are aware that the world needs millions and millions of entrepreneurs to invent the new paradigm, to scale up to large scale with acceleration. Because we need acceleration to reduce the time of the transition from the old paradigm to the new paradigm for one reason: The longer the transitions are, the higher the sacrifices will be for the current generations!

—Tugrul Atamer

ACKNOWLEDGMENTS

We, the many and varied authors of this book, are very appreciative for all of the assistance we received throughout the process of its creation. In particular, we would like to thank the World Entrepreneurship Forum and Wiley for their efforts in making this book a reality. We would also like to especially thank our families and friends for their wonderful support and encouragement throughout this process. Finally, a heartfelt thank you to Stephanie Kergall for everything she did along the way, to Mara Strauss for her excellent effort editing and proofreading, and to Spencer Strauss for his outstanding work as the lead editor for each chaper. Thank you all.

AUTHOR NOTE

What you have in your hand is the result of an extraordinary collaboration and group effort. For the past few years, as members of the World Entrepreneurship Forum, we have been sharing ideas at our yearly think tank sessions. But it has been here, in this book, where we have been able to really explore them more deeply, share them more fully, and see how they fit together.

Each chapter of this book is written by a different world-class expert in his or her field. I, as the lead author, was given the privilege (and challenge!) of tying our ideas together into a cohesive whole, and as such, you will see my introduction at the beginning of every chapter. I hope that my contributions add in some meaningful, if small, way to the insight and expertise shared by my co-authors. If we did our job right, then the whole of this book will be greater than the sum of its parts.

—Steven D. Strauss

SECTION I

The New World

CHAPTER 1

The Global Entrepreneurial Revolution

Inderjit Singh

An engineer by training, a serial entrepreneur with extensive experience, and a Member of the Singapore Parliament, Inderjit is also the co-president of the World Entrepreneurship Forum.

Whatever you can do, or dream you can, begin it.
Boldness has genius, magic, and power in it.
—Johann Wolfgang von Goethe

We are living in an amazing moment in which the world is changing, seemingly before our very eyes. Countries and leaders rise and fall. The polar ice caps melt, oceans rise, and coasts recede. Yesterday's third-world economies become today's global economic powers. It is a time of tremendous, momentous, international, transformational change.

Whether through the rise of terrorism, global warming, failing states, aging populations, persistent poverty, or social injustice, this modern, complex world can, at times, overwhelm. Some changes seem too big to be solved, intractable. And yet, simultaneously, we live in a time of tremendous transformation: Modern medicine is a marvel. The Internet has allowed us to learn almost anything and connect with almost anyone, anywhere, at any time. Democracy and the rule of law continue their forward march. Humanity's ability to adapt, adopt new ways, adjust to a changing world, and overcome great challenges is the reason the world marches forward. Many people the world over are living longer, healthier, and more productive lives.

So, to quote the great futurist Buckminster Fuller, we have a choice. Which will it be: Utopia or Oblivion? That there actually is no clear-cut answer and the many forces pulling the planet in many different, divergent directions make the challenge doubly difficult. Indeed, it is not inconceivable to foresee a time when climate change is not only beyond the point where it can be debated, but actually too far along to be solved. We may be there already. Maybe violence, poverty, terrorism, sexism, racism, ageism, and all of the other -isms that confound the world will simply prove to be too much.

Yes, we have a lot of problems. To many people, problems signify failure: proof of an inability to find a resolution. Others consider problems something to avoid altogether. And still others will refuse to notice that we have some big, deep, almost insurmountable problems to solve if we are to leave this world a better place for our children.

The operative phrase there was "almost insurmountable."

Because the good news is that there is one type of Homo sapiens who does not fear failure as much as he or she fears not trying. One sort of human who reads the litany of woes above and, instead of seeing it as an overwhelming burden to bear, chooses instead to see it as an incredible challenge to be met. These folks see pollution, poverty, a lack of cell phone coverage, and the need for a better mousetrap all as evidence of the same thing: an unmet need of one sort or another, and as such, a potential opportunity.

Say hello to the problem solvers. Say hello to the entrepreneur.

To the entrepreneur, problems are not something to be avoided or proof of failure, but rather an opportunity—maybe disguised, yes, but an opportunity nonetheless. This view, that hidden even in the biggest problem is a task to be mastered, a challenge to be overcome, a diamond in the rough, has long been shared by great leaders:

- *British Prime Minister Winston Churchill once remarked, "Difficulties mastered are opportunities won"*
- *U.S. President Harry S. Truman put it this way: "A pessimist is one who makes difficulties of his opportunities and an optimist is one who makes opportunities of his difficulties"*

• *Management guru Peter Drucker agrees: "The entrepreneur always searches for change, responds to it, and exploits it as an opportunity"*

The difference is that today, it is not just the exceptional leader who realizes that within the seeds of destruction are nuggets of gold, waiting to be discovered, capitalized upon, transformed, and utilized. No, now, here, today, there is an army, nay, a global revolution of entrepreneurs and entrepreneurship that is changing the planet—fundamentally, and for the better.

From the fall of the Berlin Wall to the disintegration of the Soviet Union to the rise of capitalism in China and throughout all of Asia to the ascent of the Internet and global e-commerce, we are witnesses today to the advent of a new age. Not only an age in which entrepreneurs are forming businesses and inventing products but, far more fundamentally, an age in which people are taking what works—the essential ideas of entrepreneurship (seeing a problem, coming up with a solution, forming a team, and serving the market)—and applying these ideas to business as well as to a vast array of social problems, so as to solve them.

Welcome to the age of the entrepreneur. Welcome to the global entrepreneurial revolution. And hang on to your hats because nothing is ever going to be the same.

■ ■ ■

The Entrepreneurial Tsunami

There are many ways to look at entrepreneurship. An entrepreneur can be defined narrowly, as someone who takes a risk with money to make money by starting a business. More broadly, entrepreneurship can be seen as an attitude through which the entrepreneur creates something out of nothing. Whether he or she engineers a new business or a new project or a new community, whether it is a money-making opportunity or otherwise, in the bigger sense, entrepreneurship involves innovation: changing the status quo to something better and helping to transform lives in the process.

Of course, it is easy to see those who start businesses as entrepreneurs but less obvious that someone who does not create a business can be an entrepreneur, but let's consider that option as well. One example of a

person we might consider a great entrepreneur who did not start a
business is the founding Prime Minister of Singapore, Mr. Lee
Kuan Yew.

Lee and his team built Singapore from nothing after the territory
gained independence from the British. From a small fishing village
without any natural resources except its people, this group of pioneering
politicians under Lee created something out of nothing—the Singapore
of today. Singapore was transformed from a third-world to a first-world
country in just one generation. This could not have been achieved
without the tenacity of an entrepreneurial team, nor without creativity
and innovation in resolving problems faced by the country, thus making
it among the richest nations in the world today. They did it by utilizing
what are thought of as capitalistic, entrepreneurial ideas and applying
them to nation building: giving incentives for achievement, harnessing
idealism and profit seeking for the common good, creating a community
invested in preferred outcomes, and all the rest.

The "I have a dream" speech delivered by American activist Dr.
Martin Luther King, Jr., on August 28, 1963, was a defining moment of
the American civil rights movement, and in his own way, Dr. King,
too, was an entrepreneur—if you think of an entrepreneur as an
innovator who challenges the status quo to change lives. In that regard
there can be no doubt that Dr. King was in fact a master entrepreneur,
and the result is that the United States today is a testament to his vision,
his dream, with no less than a black man being elected President of the
United States.

Until recently, the icons of entrepreneurship emerged from just a few
centers of the world where entrepreneurship seemed to thrive. The
Silicon Valley in Northern California is the most obvious example that
most countries have wanted to emulate, and more recently, Taiwan and
Israel have emerged as two other countries where entrepreneurship is
now thriving.

Israel created an entrepreneurial society in many ways and for several
reasons. Entrepreneurship started off in Israel as a means to economic
survival when Soviet Jews began to move to the country in the 1980s. To
help create jobs for the new immigrants, the Office of the Chief Scientist
began promoting research and development and entrepreneurship
through both its technological incubation program and seed funding.
The introduction of the $100 million Yozma program in the late 1980s

further fostered the growth of high-tech start-ups. The government also encouraged foreign corporations to come to Israel, with more than 200 of them setting up R&D facilities in the country.

This led to the employment and training of scientists and engineers, many of whom subsequently created their own tech start-ups. As a result, the general attitude towards entrepreneurship in the country changed. Today, entrepreneurship is regarded as a prestigious career choice in Israel, instead of a necessity. The general public is excited about the successes of high-tech companies listed on NASDAQ, acquired by larger companies, etc. Today, from Tel Aviv to Haifa, more and more young people prefer to work for tech start-ups than large corporations.

Similarly, Taiwan has created, through culture and government policies, a vibrant economic environment in which the entrepreneurial potential of its people is being be realized fully. A significant number of the government's strategies have focused on establishing the high-tech industry sectors, especially in electronics and semiconductors. By luring back expatriate brain power, by training more science and engineering graduates, by boosting productivity through automation, by increasing personnel training, and by fostering technological innovation, the Taiwanese government has created an entrepreneurial ecosystem and, in the process, boosted Taiwanese enterprises.

The Taiwanese have an old saying, "Better to be the head of a chicken than the tail of an ox," which describes many things, including their business ideology. It was this mentality that led to the emergence of "black hands" in the 1980s. "Black hands" learned their skills through apprenticeship in factories instead of schools, subsequently setting up their own competing firms. Being a "black hand" was and still is a source of pride for the Taiwanese people, as it was considered respectable to build one's own business through one's own effort. The result of all of this is that Taiwan has one of the highest ratios of companies to people on Planet Entrepreneur.

A Taiwanese joke describes the entrepreneurial scene perfectly: "If you throw a stone in the streets of Taipei, you are likely to hit a Chairman of the Board."

What is the common thread that runs through the Silicon Valley, Israel, Taiwan, South Korea, China, and other places around the globe where entrepreneurship is thriving? Well, it starts with a mentality. Consider the Silicon Valley in California. This area was once part of the so-called "Wild West," and it seems that that notion took root. This idea of bold risk-taking was part of the culture of the region, inspiring computer pioneers like Steve Jobs and Steve Wozniak to take risks and launch a computer revolution. By the same token, for many years, Israel and Taiwan were in a state of war, and as such, the people there developed a survivalist mentality that helped them take chances, too—for different reasons, but nevertheless eventually nurturing hubs of entrepreneurship.

Fast forward to today and what is happening around the world—whether in the North, South, East, or West. What we see is that entrepreneurship is quickly becoming the idea that is taking over and transforming the planet and is, therefore, being embraced as the way forward for most nations.

Why is that? For starters, entrepreneurship works, plain and simple. Entrepreneurs see opportunities to fill the gaps and in the process, as we say in the World Entrepreneurship Forum, become "the creators of wealth and social justice." Furthermore, as the world has become more connected, physical boundaries no longer pose a barrier to the movement of ideas, capital, and talent. As the world opens up, new opportunities arise. We are increasingly being exposed to what is happening outside our home countries and learning about how entrepreneurship has helped shape and improve lives, whether in the United States, China, India, Singapore, Denmark, or wherever.

Maybe most importantly, in this interconnected e-world, there is a heightened awareness that entrepreneurs are the change-makers. They create value. We see them make things happen. And as such, more and more people are beginning to realize that maybe, just maybe, they can do it too. So, whether it is improving the political situation in one's country, creating a new business, or working to better the lives of the disadvantaged and marginalized, the entrepreneurial mind-set is sweeping the planet.

The Entrepreneur

Entrepreneurship has been defined and described in many different ways. The term *entrepreneur* originates from a French word and is commonly used to describe an individual who organizes and operates a business or businesses, taking on financial risk to do so. Other definitions include:

Joseph Schumpeter: "Entrepreneurs are innovators who use a process of shattering the status quo of the existing products and services, to set up new products, new services."

Peter Drucker: "An entrepreneur searches for change, responds to it and exploits opportunities. Innovation is a specific tool of an entrepreneur hence an effective entrepreneur converts a source into a resource."

Howard Stevenson: "Entrepreneurship is the pursuit of opportunity without regard to resources currently controlled."

Depending on the type of business, where and when it is conducted, and the person running the show, entrepreneurial activities and outcomes can differ greatly. The McDonald brothers were running a successful microenterprise, a diner selling burgers and fries, just like any other. However, the vision and leadership of Ray Kroc turned McDonald's into a scalable, high-growth fast-food giant. On the other end of the entrepreneurial spectrum is an organization like Ashoka:

> When Bill Drayton started Ashoka, he knew that the old ways of dealing with social problems—through the public sector, charity, or too often by simply ignoring them—were by and large failures. But he also knew that creative, driven, innovative problem-solvers in communities all over the world were quietly rolling up their sleeves and getting the work done.
>
> Ashoka started off by finding these unheralded local heroes and, through an especially rigorous selection process, offering them fellowships. The fellowship stipend and support (often provided through partnerships with private-sector firms, such as the management consulting firm McKinsey & Company) helped catapult these heroes' proven solutions to become self-sustaining and system-changing.
>
> Most of us associate entrepreneurship with the business world; the invention of new ways of doing things has, in our lifetime, mostly happened in the service of profit-making ventures. Today that's changing. More and more people with entrepreneurial spirit and creativity are putting their talents and ambition to work solving social problems and creating systems to support their solutions' growth. Ashoka has been a leader in this movement for three decades now, providing fellowships to

those innovators who truly stand out for their promise to transform entire
sectors. (Ashoka.org)

So clearly, vision and leadership are also part of any entrepreneurial
equation.

Another truth is that entrepreneurship is a risk venture. According to
the University of Tennessee research, an average of 25 percent of start-
ups fail within the first year. The path of an entrepreneur is fraught with
obstacles and challenges, and it is not uncommon for one to meet with
multiple failures before achieving success. So to be an entrepreneur, you
must have a high degree of risk tolerance.

Entrepreneurship also involves uncertainty. Leaving the job and the
benefits to start a new venture is exciting, yes, but equally, success is
uncertain. That uncertainty extends to the market, as, often, entrepreneurs are looking to sell people something before they even know they
might need it. But if you hit that bull's eye, the rewards can be very sweet
indeed. Whether it is Apple's iPhone or simply a small business that grows
and hires, succeeding in an uncertain world is both financially and
emotionally rewarding. Having clarity of a vision therefore is what helps
an entrepreneur navigate through all the uncertainty.

Entrepreneurship also requires creating value from limited resources.
Most entrepreneurs have finite resources, be they money, time, or
manpower. The magic happens when they are able to use those precious
resources to create a product or service that people want and are willing
to pay for. Take Sara Blakely, founder and inventor of Spanx, for
example. After her "aha" moment (fed up with them showing under
her pants, she cut off the feet of her pantyhose before going onstage for a
stand-up comedy gig), she started her multimillion-dollar hosiery empire
right in the back of her one-bedroom apartment. Her mother drafted the
original product drawing for the Spanx patent, and Blakely secured her
first sale to Neiman Marcus by giving her own personal "before and after"
demonstration.

The Once and Future of Entrepreneurship

To understand just how big this global entrepreneurial revolution
actually is and to see how it is shaping almost every area of modern
life, it would behoove us to have a better understanding of how we got

here. Yet to sum up in a few paragraphs how entrepreneurship has changed and developed over time would be like trying to condense Darwin's 1859 book on the theory of evolution, *On the Origin of Species*, into a two-minute elevator pitch. Tough, but we will try.

In ancient times, entrepreneurship was a simple concept that ensured survival. Barter and trade enabled farmers to exchange excess goods for items that were essential but low in supply. This simple exercise forced people to think about the value of goods in terms of supply and demand: Things that were scarce or rare were highly valued, much like the diamond is today.

However, in the thirteenth century, merchant-traveler Marco Polo found a new way to exploit the concept of value. During his famous 24-year attempt to establish trade routes to China, Polo signed contracts with merchants who would act as the equivalent of our modern-day "middle man," taking 25 percent of their profits as commission. This was the beginning of assigning an exchange value to goods and services.

According to Biography.com, "Marco Polo was born in 1254, in Venice, Italy. He traveled extensively with his family, journeying from Europe to Asia from 1271 to 1295. He remained in China for 17 of those years. Around 1292, he left China, acting as consort along the way to a Mongol princess who was being sent to Persia." Upon his return to Italy, Polo was imprisoned, and he dictated his famous book, *Il Milione*, which describes his travels and experiences, to a cellmate. The book and his travels influenced adventurers and merchants far and wide, including Christopher Columbus.

Entrepreneurs in the Middle Ages were much more conservative and risk-averse. Entrepreneurs who prevailed during this age tended to be stonemasons, craftsmen, and builders. Like Michelangelo, the skilled architect behind St. Peter's Basilica, or Da Vinci, entrepreneurs then were people who used their skills to create value in a personalized manner.

The eighteenth and nineteenth centuries were the invention-led eras of entrepreneurship. The Industrial Revolution led to life-changing products like the steam engine, light bulbs, and the telephone. Entrepreneurship was often no longer about selling a product to meet current needs, but envisioning a market, creating new demands, and finding technological solutions to meet them.

The twentieth century saw the first real swells in the transformational global entrepreneurial tsunami that was to come. A generation to be shaped by world wars, the entrepreneurs of the 1900s began to use entrepreneurship as a creative means of marketing and selling their products to rebuild nations and create jobs. Henry Ford's Model T was the epitome of mass manufacturing and mass marketing back then. With his vision of making automobiles an accessible commodity to the man on the street (and creating a middle class who could afford them to boot), Ford invented the assembly line to produce cars quickly and cheaply. By 1914, Ford's company had a whopping 48 percent of the automobile industry.

And yet, this brief overview is just that—brief. It is by no means a comprehensive account of entrepreneurship and it is not meant to be. What we are trying to point out here is that entrepreneurs are ever-changing, adapting to the situation at hand, are versatile and resilient, and take on many shapes and forms.

Yesterday's entrepreneurs are not the same as today's, and today's won't be the same as tomorrow's. That is the excitement and challenge of entrepreneurship. Aside from hoping to profit from the Next Big Thing, today's entrepreneurs are also using the many and varied tools in the entrepreneurial tool chest to solve a wide variety of global problems, from creating clean sanitation for the world's poor to figuring out how to bring electricity to rural India. With each directional change in history, you see a new breed of entrepreneurs adapt and thrive in the new environment, becoming the Davids willing to challenge the Goliaths. In time, they will become the Goliaths and will eventually be taken down by the new breed of Davids. This is the circle of life. This is natural selection. This is evolution. This is entrepreneurship.

The Global Entrepreneurial Revolution

Especially in the past 20 years or so, the entrepreneurship scene has taken a very interesting turn. Because of a confluence of factors and key events, we have seen entrepreneurial activity explode in regions previously dominated by large private or public corporations. New revolutionary industries like social media, casual gaming, and big data analytics have sprung up seemingly overnight and are garnering billions of dollars of investor monies, creating millions of jobs, and encouraging many more to join the entrepreneurial ranks.

Why is entrepreneurship exploding now? What factors make the global entrepreneurial revolution a possibility? The exponential growth of entrepreneurial activity and the incredible pace at which things are changing can be credited to several factors:

- **Technology advancements:** Throughout the ages, the role of technology in entrepreneurship has been huge. The Industrial Revolution came about with the invention of the steam engine, and the products and business that resulted changed the world. Today, it is the Internet that is transforming the way we communicate, learn, share and disseminate information, and work. It has changed the way we live and will continue to do so. In each one of these eras, entrepreneurs have taken advantage of these radical developments and have used them to create businesses that are innovative, differentiated, and sometimes even global.

Milaap, a social enterprise headquartered in Singapore, enables anyone in the world to lend money to the working poor in India so they can get access to education, clean water, safe lighting and more. In the past, the only access to funding and help these individuals had was through traditional sources like banks, nonprofit organizations (Red Cross, etc.), and the government. With the help of the Internet, an online payment portal (PayPal), and social media platforms to create awareness (Facebook and Twitter in particular), Milaap directly connects underprivileged individuals (or small groups) in India with potential lenders located in affluent countries like the United Kingdom, the United States, and Singapore. Via regular updates and repayment progress reports, lenders can see the immediate impact their money has made. This is the new face of entrepreneurship.

- **Giants and their "fall":** In most countries, we see the "queen bee" effect—a hive of entrepreneurial activity supporting large multinational corporations. However, today, it is the exact opposite that is true. The Great Recession and the resulting failure or restructuring of large companies led to the creation of many small businesses. It is akin to the feeding frenzy that we see when a whale dies, resulting in the renewal of the ecosystem. That same kind of renewal in the entrepreneurship system is occurring today. When giant corporations like Kodak or Lehman Brothers fail, they release talented individuals, some of whom, out of either necessity or preference, stay out of the corporate cubicles to start their own little empires. Restructuring also created opportunities for new companies in outsourcing. As a company gets larger, overhead goes up and the company relies increasingly on outsourcing to minimize cost. Corporate downsizing and economic restructuring are therefore major contributors to the rise of entrepreneurship.
- **"Open for business":** In the past two decades, emerging markets like India, Brazil, and Indonesia have embraced entrepreneurship and taken on a larger portion of the world's GDP and are playing a more important role in the driving the world's economy. Of course, the most salient example of the power of entrepreneurship can be seen in China, which went from being the world's eleventh largest economy in 1990 to its second largest in 2010. Indeed, the story of China's capitalist turn is one of the greatest entrepreneurial lessons in the history of the planet. By turning its collective back on communism and opening its proverbial door for business, China unleashed an entrepreneurship epidemic that spread throughout the land, creating millions of businesses in less than a generation. In fact, China's embrace of entrepreneurship has not only lifted millions of people out of poverty, it has created the largest middle class the world has ever seen.

With the incredible example of China leading the way, emerging countries like Cambodia and Vietnam are also opening up and embracing capitalism. The resulting tidal wave of entrepreneurship will only keep building, spreading, and flooding the world.

Now at this point, an astute reader might be thinking, "Wait, how is this revolutionary? Aren't today's entrepreneurs just adapting to the environment, to the trends and circumstances they see around them, just as they always have?"

No. This is different.

We believe that the entrepreneurial revolution is not only technological, not only global, not only accessible to all, but additionally lies in the transformation of the mindset of entrepreneurship—from fulfilling one's livelihood needs to making a difference and solving problems in today's world. The phenomenal rise of social entrepreneurship, which combines the making of money with doing good, attests to this. No longer is entrepreneurship just about the chasing of profit (though it is of course about that too), additionally, it is about the chasing of opportunities and a love for adventure. Entrepreneurship is no longer in the hands of just a few opportunistic people, it is in the hands of the masses, who increasingly are using it to change the world.

This is not your father's entrepreneur.

Social Entrepreneurship

Another major driver of the entrepreneurial revolution that is transforming the world is social entrepreneurship. Attracting everyone from Bill Gates to Sir Richard Branson to small, local entrepreneurs, social entrepreneurship is vital to understanding the global entrepreneurial revolution. The key elements of social entrepreneurship are these:

- Social entrepreneurs run organizations that are focused on social objectives, not profit per se. For example, a restaurant might be run by special-needs employees. There, it is the training and opportunity being provided, not the profit, that is the important thing. Entrepreneurship is a means to an end.
- In government, new legislation and incentives are being developed to support social issues and promote social entrepreneurship. Thus, not only GDP growth but also socially sustainable growth is emphasized.
- In the area of finance, there is talk of social stock markets and socially responsible investing.
- Finally, in the area of philanthropy, we are seeing many wealthy people now supporting social entrepreneurial activities.

Transforming Government's Role

The economic turmoil we have seen in the past few years has also spurred public leaders to refocus their efforts to encourage entrepreneurship. After the economic upheaval hit in 2008, government officials around the world had to grapple with massive unemployment and mounting public debt. Central banks had to jump into the fray to prop up failing giant corporations in a bid to stem the tide. With jobs slow to return to the market and economic uncertainty still looming in many developed and developing countries, many governments began to rely on local entrepreneurs to restart the economic engines.

The role of government cannot be underestimated when it comes to nurturing—or killing—entrepreneurship. A stable, transparent, pro-business government is critical to ensuring the success of a business, while an unpredictable political environment can wreak havoc for business owners. Apart from the usual suspects of low corporate tax rates and fees, established legal and financial structures to support businesses, and proper infrastructure like roads, public transport, and telecommunication networks to provide a conducive environment for businesses and entrepreneurs, what more can a government do? For that, let's take a look at some of the more progressive governments around the world for some ideas:

Singapore: Singapore has done a great job of creating a pro-enterprise environment and increasing access to finance. Ranked as the easiest place to do business for six years straight by the World Bank, Singapore's public sector has stepped up efforts to create infrastructure and support systems for start-ups and aspiring entrepreneurs since late 2012.

For example, seeing the need to create a space for entrepreneurs to interact and grow sustainably, Singapore's public sector collaborated with large corporations and local education institutions to create Block 71, an old industrial building retrofitted to be a start-up hub. With growing vigor, more start-ups, private incubators, and venture capital funds have moved into the space, creating a breeding ground for innovation, creativity, and excitement about starting up.

Singapore has also created knowledge and network systems through the union of a group of entrepreneurs and the public sector, otherwise known as the Action Community for Entrepreneurship

(ACE). With programs that match start-ups in their first year to willing mentors, ACE attempts to create a mentoring relationship that will last. These freshly minted start-ups are then plugged into the Singaporean entrepreneurship community through ACE's networking platforms.

To keep the ecosystem of start-up support going, the public sector also provides grants and co-investment schemes to develop incubators, seed start-up stage investments, and incentivize venture-capital investments. The goal is not just to seed and grow start-ups, but to ensure that the private sector is being encouraged to do so too.

New Zealand: New Zealand is ranked the number-one country in which to start a business in the Doing Business 2013 survey by the World Bank. Amazingly, it only takes one procedure, one day, and no minimum paid-in capital to start a business there. Compare this to Venezuela, where you have to go through 17 procedures and wait an average of 144 days to register a company.

Access to capital is also, of course, a main concern for start-ups. New Zealand's public sector gets this. They have created grants to develop everything from management capabilities to founder's capabilities. They also help to seed the creation of intellectual property through funding up to half of research and development costs. Government programs will even fund an intern to assist with your R&D project. New Zealand also has a Flexi-Wage scheme through which new business owners can apply for an allowance from the government—a sort of pay from the public sector to lower the opportunity cost of quitting that job and starting a new business.

Private Support of Entrepreneurship

Remember when people had to hit up their friends and family for start-up capital? Or they took on two jobs just to sock away enough money to start their own business? If they were persistent, they could get some face time with a banker to convince him or her that their idea was worth a loan. And if they were really fortunate, they might catch the eye of a big-time investor or venture capital fund manager who was willing to take a gamble on them. Well, things have changed a lot. Sure, getting funding can still be very tough for entrepreneurs, but the good news is that there have been major changes in the way entrepreneurs access funding. New (and old) options abound.

After the dotcom bust, venture capital funds and private equity firms pulled back, but today they are investing again. With deeper pockets and increased risk appetites, professional private capital is increasingly available to entrepreneurs. This is evidenced by the surge in start-up conferences, pitching events, competitions, investor networking sessions, and venture-capital open houses. Events like TechCrunch, Startup Demo Day, and South By Southwest (SXSW) are becoming critical for tech entrepreneurs. The purpose of such events is the same—to bring buyers, sellers, investors, and investees together to create businesses and economic activity.

A new way that entrepreneurs are getting funded is via crowdfunding (see Chapter 9). By leveraging the power of the Internet, entrepreneurs kill two birds with one stone: First of all, they can get instant validation of their business idea from the "crowd," and secondly, if their business makes sense, they get funding from strangers around the world.

Since 2009, Kickstarter.com has helped fund over 40,000 projects by raising over $612 million from more than 4 million people.

So How Does This Impact You?

Assuming that you picked up this book because you are an entrepreneur, or aspire to be one, this section is probably the most important part of the chapter for you. While it is good to understand how things have changed over the years and the factors leading up to the state of entrepreneurship today, it is infinitely more valuable to know how the global entrepreneurial revolution impacts you as an entrepreneur.

First of all, things are going to be easier. With both the public and private sectors taking entrepreneurship more seriously, it is no wonder that many more people are taking the plunge and starting their own businesses. Governments around the world have also been improving policies and procedures to ensure fair business practices and ease of doing business. We have also seen instances in which governments are stepping up to play an active role in pushing for a vibrant entrepreneurial community, and that is all very good for entrepreneurs like you.

With an increasing amount of resources and thought being poured into encouraging and helping entrepreneurship, it is much easier to get seed funding for your business. Both private and public sector monies being poured into this space have grown exponentially.

Technology of course is also playing a major part and making entrepreneurship easier than ever. Not only has it made funding more accessible to entrepreneurs, it has also helped build a thriving community of entrepreneurs both online and offline. The Internet has brought entrepreneurs around the world closer together, making the tough and sometimes lonely journey of an entrepreneur much easier. Knowing that you are not alone in your struggle is great. Having a mentor to guide you is even better. And finding a partner or investor halfway around the world may be best of all. It happens every day, and it is thanks to technology.

Additionally, now, the world is your market. Most companies can be global from day one. You too, no matter how big or small your business, can be a global business. The market you can sell to is both borderless and limited only by your imagination and appetite.

And yet, things are going to be tougher, too; there are two sides to every coin. Just as technology has opened borders and entrepreneurship's friendly rules have made it easier for you to join the entrepreneurship party, these changes have also caused many more to veer away from a corporate career to become their own boss. The entrepreneurial world is fast becoming a very crowded space, in which it is getting increasingly hard to survive. Lured by the promise of riches and self-fulfillment coupled with the relative ease of starting a business, many people have rushed headlong into entrepreneurship only to find themselves on steep cliffs and uphill climbs, competing for limited footholds with scores of other climbers.

Not everyone survives and succeeds. But, that said, there are more resources, more help, and more options than ever. Sure, entrepreneurship is a challenge, but if it weren't, it wouldn't be as much fun.

A good place to go to start your entrepreneurial journey is TheSelfEmployed.com.

Through crowdfunding, social media marketing, and the disintegration of the value chain of businesses (i.e., your supply chain occurs in different countries), the world has become a much smaller and better connected place. Entrepreneurs can access resources, capabilities, and markets much more easily than they could at any time in the past. Consumers are now participating in companies even before a product is created and strangers are willing to fund projects at the click of a button. The world is changing and changing fast. With so many participants, the entrepreneurship revolution is set to explode.

Bottom line: This is an incredible time for entrepreneurship and therefore an incredible time to be an entrepreneur. If others can do it, so can you, and you can do it now. Remember this: No time is right or wrong to pursue your dreams. Follow your heart, look for a good idea, create a great team, use technology to your advantage, and go change your world and the world. It is time to join the new entrepreneurial revolution.

■ ■ ■

 **Inderjit Singh** is a serial entrepreneur, a member of the Singapore Parliament, and Co-President of the World Entrepreneurship Forum. He has started 11 companies around the world, of which six are successful, two are still in the process of growing, and three have failed. He built multimillion-dollar companies, including high-tech companies, from scratch and is considered the foremost champion of entrepreneurship in Singapore. He is the author of *The Art and Science of Entrepreneurship.* Inderjit is also an inventor, with three patents to his name.

CHAPTER 2

The Entrepreneurial Technological Transformation

Nikhil Agarwal

Nikhil Agarwal is President of Cambridge Global Partners (CGP) and a researcher at the University of Edinburgh. Previously, he was the Professor of Management and the Founding Director of Europe Asia Business School.

It's more fun to be a pirate than to join the Navy.

—Steve Jobs

We are entering into, indeed have entered into, a new era in which entrepreneurship is becoming a driving force on the planet. It drives economies and innovation, it fuels dreams and ventures, and it creates connections and understanding. In a world where there are many, many divergent forces attempting to foster dissention, a powerful force like entrepreneurship (and an economic one to boot) is a necessary and welcome counterbalance. Indeed, when it seems like the world is splintering ever more into smaller and smaller factions, religions, tribes, and peoples—all demanding their rights, proclaiming their autonomy, and nursing their grudges—one of the few forces actually creating a better world, via businesses, products, innovation, communication, and inter-dependency—a force that stresses our commonalities over our differences—is entrepreneurship.

And just how are entrepreneurs doing that? What are the tools that enable us to rise above the din?

Technology.

We are living during one of the greatest technological revolutions of any era, and entrepreneurs are both making that possible and taking advantage of the opportunities technology provides. Technology has made it so that anyone, anywhere, can start their own business, lead their own cause, organize their own community, and rally their own troops. It has radically brought down the cost of entry into the global marketplace; has made it so that any business, no matter how small, can look as big as their biggest competitor (at least online!); and has enabled millions of people to live a better life.

The global entrepreneurial revolution is possible because the global technological revolution is the engine that makes it go.

■ ■ ■

We checked into this new century only a decade back. Although the twenty-first century has brought with it many of the challenges of the old century, it has not, as of yet, offered many solutions. But that said, it is highly likely, even probable, that the solutions that we will see in this new century will be developed not by a political or religious or social leader, but instead by a technology entrepreneur. After all, already, it is the technology entrepreneurs who have created the social networks that are changing how people live, share, speak, shop, and organize. It is the technology entrepreneur who has made the mobile phone the most used tool in the world, connecting billions. And it is the technology entrepreneur who is harnessing the power of the waves and the sun and the atom to create cleaner, more sustainable energy. It is the technology entrepreneur who is most influential in shaping and changing the world.

The very idea of a technology entrepreneur has evolved as times have changed—from the Industrial Revolution to the Commercial Revolution and on to the Information Revolution. Not long ago, entrepreneurs were industrialists and factory owners. Then, during the Commercial Revolution, they were shopkeepers and storeowners. Now, in the Internet era, entrepreneurs are innovators and collaborators. And given the changing demographics of the planet, it is not inconceivable that the next entrepreneurial wave will be a social innovation revolution led by people who are living on the fringe.

In fact, in this century, what we will likely see are ecologically aware, Internet-driven, socially connected transformational entrepreneurs, people who will rise above the noise and give us solid techno-social solutions to solve real-world problems in a sustainable and systematic manner. The underlying philosophy of the World Entrepreneurship Forum is that entrepreneurs are creators of wealth and social justice. We believe that transformational entrepreneurship, whether big or small, is the way forward for our planet. And we know that such a transformation will very likely emerge from new entrepreneurs who create and use new technologies to share new ideas and solutions that dare to challenge the old ways. That, in fact, is what we mean by the entrepreneurial technological transformation.

In this chapter, we will discuss how technology entrepreneurs have influenced our world and will continue to do so at an accelerated rate. The original technology entrepreneurs of last century, the Internet entrepreneur of today, and the so-called "frugal" entrepreneurs of tomorrow have creatively expanded horizons to build the smarter solutions.

Tech Entrepreneurs 1.0

Just who and what is a technology entrepreneur? While today we consider Internet CEOs to be the prototypical technology entrepreneur, this of course was not always the case. And it is important that we have a broader understanding of the term *technology* so that we are not limited by today's somewhat narrow view of the term. Technology is not just about computers. Two of the most famous technology entrepreneurs ever were Thomas Edison and George Eastman. They were inventors, successful businessmen, and great philanthropists—true transformational leaders and the forerunners of the technological entrepreneurs of today.

Consider the great Thomas Alva Edison, one of the most influential figures of the last millennium. Edison had 1,093 U.S. patents to his name. His most recognized inventions were the light bulb, the phonograph, and the Kinetoscope—a small box for viewing moving films. He also contributed to improving the design of the stock ticker, the telegraph, and Alexander Graham Bell's telephone. Edison was famously quoted as saying, "Genius is 1 percent inspiration and 99 percent perspiration." He was also quoted to have said, "I have not failed. I've just found 10,000 ways that won't work." His biggest gift, aside from his technological genius of course, was his ability to maximize profits by mass production of his own inventions. Edison had a remarkable ability to invent, to sell, and to be an entrepreneur. These abilities led him to found 14 companies (including General Electric) that are still in existence today.

At the age of 14, Edison was totally deaf in his left ear and approximately 80 percent deaf in his right ear. Like any true entrepreneur, Edison found an advantage in his challenge, realizing that his deafness helped him to concentrate on his work without being distracted.

Edison and George Eastman (of Eastman Kodak fame) were good friends and also business partners. Eastman was the visionary inventor who made photography an amateur's sport. In 1900, this revolutionary technical entrepreneur introduced the "Brownie" camera for just $1; it was preloaded with enough film for 100 exposures and after all the shots were taken, the camera was returned for processing to the Kodak central processing center in New York. The camera with its film replaced was returned to the customer along with the prints. It was an easy, efficient, and profitable operation.

Aside from creating a system that ensured repeat sales and customers (a significant feat in its own right), Eastman was also an early branding guru, long before the term *branding* had been invented. He believed a product's name should not come from some dictionary definition; instead, it should be unique and associated with the product alone. So Eastman coined the term *Kodak* because he thought it was easy to remember and difficult to misspell. He was one of the few inventors ever who understood both technology and marketing and was able to marry the two (the mantle later taken up by the great Steve Jobs). Eastman was also a generous philanthropist who donated over $75 million for projects, including gifts to MIT, the Eastman School of Music in 1918, and the University of Rochester School of Medicine and Dentistry in 1921.

Technological entrepreneurship in the early twentieth century like that of Edison and Eastman was not easy. Entrepreneurship and innovation were not nearly as widespread as they are today, and moreover, the world was painfully divided into capitalist and communist

Kodak has also been credited with inventing some of the most memorable marketing slogans of our time, including:
"You press the button, we do the rest"
"Brownie Camera: Operated by any school boy or girl"
"A Kodak moment"
"Great photos start with great film, choose Kodak"

blocs with limited trade interaction between the two. But with the collapse of communism in the Soviet Bloc, which paved the way for the creation of a free market economy in former communist countries, technology entrepreneurs in the late twentieth century began to influence the developing world significantly. Countries like India, China, and Brazil were persuaded to open their economies to rapid technological industrialization. By the end of the twentieth century, industrialization slowly moved away from western economies toward developing economies. Eventually, the development of the Internet and information technology (IT) in the late twentieth century created a more entrepreneurial, international, and collaborative way of doing business.

Thus, and not surprisingly, the next generation of great technological transformational leaders became known as the Internet entrepreneurs. It is these Internet entrepreneurs who are today the leading forces of the global entrepreneurial revolution, creating businesses and platforms that are being used by billions and inspiring a new generation to do the same.

Tech Entrepreneurs 2.0

These days, a young, smiling Internet entrepreneur is everybody's darling (stock traders especially love them). They are the rocks stars of this new tech era—Steve Jobs, Bill Gates, Mark Zuckerberg, Larry Page, Sergey Brin, Jerry Yang, Jack Dorsey, Jimmy Wales, Pierre Omidyar, and the beat goes on and on. While these prominent tech entrepreneurs have generated billions of dollars' worth of enterprise value in a short span of time, maybe more important (to them and to us) is that they have changed the world for the better. Today, because of their pioneering technological entrepreneurial efforts, the world is smarter, wealthier, and more connected (and, well, just maybe sharing a tad too much).

The dot-com era is a relatively new phenomenon. It had a humble beginning on March 15, 1985, when the first dot-com company was registered by a computer manufacturer based in Cambridge, Massachusetts, called Symbolics, Inc. That year, only five other companies applied for a dot-com name. Over the next 10 years, the dot-com world witnessed slow but steady growth. By 1992, 15,000 dot-coms were registered; this grew to 1 million registered names by 1997, and it was that year that the dot-com geyser started to gush oil. The next year, 20 million new domain names were registered. Today there are over 250 million domain names registered around the world, and the Internet has changed everything it has touched—from books to money to sex to entrepreneurship. New markets have provided new opportunities for new businesses. Small companies can be global businesses now and big companies can have a more friendly small-business look via social media. Companies have changed their business models from "bricks" to "bricks 'n' clicks." And it is all because of the technology entrepreneur.

An Internet entrepreneur is defined as somebody who uses the Internet as his principal medium for doing business, customer interactions, product innovation, and transactions. Internet businesses can be completely online (Google, Facebook) or online–offline (Amazon). Facebook has over 1 billion registered users. In the history of mankind, no single product or service has been able to generate such extensive interest from such a large population. Internet companies can be big or small; some are run out of an extra room, others require massive amounts of venture capital, but all are run by Internet entrepreneurs.

Steve Jobs and Bill Gates are considered to be the two founding fathers of the computer revolution, although whether their respective companies will continue to wield the influence they have in the Internet era remains to be seen. The genuine success for Microsoft came in the pre-Internet era, circa 1995, with the introduction of the Windows 95 operating system. The Apple turnaround started with the introduction of the iPod and its seamless integration with iTunes. There were many other celebrated stories during the last 20 years of Internet domination, but the true czars of the Internet boom now are Google founders Larry Page and Sergey Brin and Facebook founder Mark Zuckerberg. These are today's top tech titans.

Generating $50 billion in annual revenue, Google's shadow now reaches well beyond the mountains of search. Indeed, Google's ad revenue has enabled the company to vastly diversify its interests, and so too have the founders diversified their own interests, investing heavily in new technologies like smart automotive and space technology. Yet they know that success can be fickle in this fast-moving, tech-driven world. Sergey Brin has been quoted as saying, "Some say Google is God. Others say Google is Satan. But if they think Google is too powerful, remember that with search engines unlike other companies, all it takes is a single click to go to another search engine." This is a great lesson for budding entrepreneurs: Success is rational. Don't allow success to rule you; you should rule success.

Google's "Ten things we know to be true":

1. Focus on the user and all else will follow
2. It's best to do one thing really, really well
3. Fast is better than slow
4. Democracy on the web works
5. You don't need to be at your desk to need an answer
6. You can make money without doing evil
7. There's always more information out there
8. The need for information crosses all borders
9. You can be serious without a suit
10. Great just isn't good enough

Mark Zuckerberg's story is like a movie script—say, *The Social Network*. He initially created a service called Facemash that allowed students to vote on the photos of their fellow students to select the "hottest" student on Harvard University campus. But Facemash closed after Zuckerberg was asked to take the website down by the university administration, and so he morphed it into "The Facebook" (with a little help from his friends). Facebook of course is now a far more sophisticated business, but the interesting thing to note from a user's perspective is that it is an entirely free tool for social networking and connection. Think about that: The technology revolution is so revolutionary that one of its biggest success stories provides its service completely free of cost. Not surprisingly, the IPO of Facebook generated $100 billion in shareholder value in 2012.

Steve Jobs and Bill Gates were "frenemies" from the start and had a love/hate relationship for many years before Jobs's untimely death in 2011. Yet despite their rivalry and disputes, over the years, these two computer giants developed a deep respect for each other's work. Regarding Steve Jobs's death, Bill Gates said, "We were within a year of the same age, and we were kind of naively optimistic and built big companies. And every fantasy we had about creating products and learning new things—we achieved all of it, and most of it as rivals. But we always retained a certain respect and communication, including even when he was sick."

The upshot is that today, "technology" seems almost to be synonymous with "the Internet," and so it probably goes without saying that Internet companies account for 25 percent of venture capital dollars now. But the fact is, it is not just the Internet that constitutes technology today. No, a whole host of other industries make up the entrepreneurial technological revolution, and as such, other tech companies in industries as diverse as energy, media, and biotech have seen significant investments from venture capitalists in the last decade.

Tech Entrepreneurs 3.0

Needless to say, becoming a tech entrepreneur like Bill Gates or Mark Zuckerberg is highly, highly unlikely. But that doesn't mean that most other tech entrepreneurs are any less ambitious or capable. They just may be a little smaller, that's all. Indeed, with so many resources available to entrepreneurs today, the problems they choose to solve and the businesses they choose to create may be no less interesting and valuable than their more famous, bigger, high-tech business cousins. Again, it may just be the size of the endeavor that's different.

Consider: As the night falls, it is pitch dark in Khamtala—50 kilometers from Gadchiroli district in the Maharashtra state in India. Electricity is in short supply; in fact, it is available only a few hours a day, and even then mainly to run irrigation pumps. Most village homes remain without electricity when they need it the most—in the evenings. Enter Kisan,[1] an entrepreneur who has found a unique way to bring light to Khamtala households.

Supported by a local nongovernmental organization (NGO), Kisan has set up a "frugal" entrepreneurial venture—a solar lantern-charging station that earns a profit, solves a problem, and alleviates a social need all in one. Reusable battery-powered lanterns are distributed by the NGO to village residents and the NGO has also trained Kisan to repair and maintain the lanterns. To work, the lanterns need physical charging at a high-powered charging station for four to five hours every day. Kisan earns his money by physically charging the lanterns at the custom-designed, solar panel–powered charging station. The charging station is set up at Kisan's house, where solar panels have been installed on his roof. Villagers drop their drained solar lanterns at Kisan's charging station every morning when they leave for work and pick them up in the evening on their way back home. Villagers pay two rupees per charge ($0.05) to recharge the solar lanterns. At the station, Kisan is able to charge about 75 lanterns per day, earning around 150 rupees for himself. Now, he is contemplating setting up solar-powered streetlights in the village to solve the problem of darkness. Through this frugal yet technologically sustainable idea, the village gets light in the evening and Kisan, the frugal entrepreneur, generates a continuous income for himself.

So-called small-scale, frugal innovation is fast becoming a trend among not only small, local entrepreneurs but also global giants like Unilever, Procter & Gamble, Tata, and Renault. The frugal innovation concept is inspired by emerging markets like India—in the Hindi language it is called "Jugaar" (joo-gaar), which literally means "work-around method" or "improvised solution to fix a problem." Navi Radjou and Jaideep Prabhu discussed frugal innovation in their book *Jugaad*

---

[1] Story based on actual events. Name and place changed on the request of the interviewee/ NGO.

Innovation: Think Frugal, Be Flexible, Generate Breakthrough Growth. According to the authors, frugal innovation is a whole new mindset; it is a paradigm shift in technology, entrepreneurship, and thinking that implements grass-roots innovation at both the local and corporate level. It is important to understand that "frugality" in this context should not be confused with business "cost-cutting" or being "penny wise and pound foolish." Frugality here means being smart and savvy, working to build world-class products with minimal cost and sell them at affordable prices with high volumes.

There are many reasons why we need sustainable, cost-effective, smart, frugal solutions and businesses, but a major one is overpopulation. According to experts, if the global population were to follow an average American lifestyle, only 1.5 billion people could live in this world. The average Western European lifestyle could be supported for only 4 billion people. The average Asian lifestyle could be supported for nearly 10 billion people, and if everyone were to follow the average African lifestyle, the earth would have enough resources for 15 billion people. But given that the world's population is about 7.1 billion in 2013 and is predicted to grow to 10 billion by 2050 and to 16 billion by 2100, the need for smart, frugal innovation and entrepreneurship should be obvious. Given that we cannot just sit, think, and do nothing and that we alone are responsible for our problems of food, energy, housing, health, and education, it is clear that we need to develop solutions through new technological advancements and innovations.

This then prompts the question: Do we need more innovators like Steve Jobs in the world, people who create billions of dollars' worth of high-tech shareholder value, or do we need more frugal, low-tech entrepreneurs like Kisan? At the World Entrepreneurship Forum, we think that we need both. We need high tech *and* low tech. We need first-world tech *and* third-world tech. We need big tech and small tech and green tech and new tech. We need today's tech and tomorrow's tech, too. We need it all.

And in both the developed and the developing world, we are getting it all, for all sorts of reasons. The last financial crisis has taught us hard lessons stemming from lackluster growth prospects, with unemployment rates rising to 27 percent in certain Western European industrialized nations. Furthermore, the need for energy, water, and other natural resources is putting increasing pressure on the environment and that in turn increases demands for frugal, sustainable, technological business models. So now we are witness to a surge of low-cost innovative technological solutions:

In Kenya, IBM is setting up an R&D lab to solve big challenges like transportation by using computer algorithms. Here's how it will work: IBM will use data from 36 installed webcams in Nairobi city streets to identify traffic patterns, plug those into its algorithm, and then use the data to send Twitter updates to drivers. Or what about this: The Tata Swach water filter can clean 3000 liters of water without electricity or running water. It uses the sophisticated technology (developed in collaboration with MIT) using rice husks and silver nanoparticles. The cost of this cutting-edge yet frugal product is 50 percent less than that of its nearest competitor.

Embrace is a U.S. firm that has developed an innovative, low-cost infant warmer for vulnerable babies. Over 20 million low-birth-weight babies are born every year around the world, and over 4 million die within their first month of life. A sleeping bag–style infant warmer aids in temperature regulation and maintaining the constant temperature over a long period. Embrace infant warmers cost a fraction of the price of other existing solutions and function without a continuous supply of electricity. This frugal solution maintains premature and low birth weight babies' body temperature to help them survive and thrive.

EcoLife is a German company that has developed environmentally friendly technology for building panels used in low-cost housing. These panels are built from agriculture waste fibers that are typically burned for disposal. The revolutionary building panels are 100 percent natural and recyclable. Using its own technology, EcoLife built a 3,000-square-meter production facility in Germany using a combination of recycled and low-energy material, including strawboard panels, in 80 days flat. The building won the World Award for Sustainable Energy from the Energy Globe Foundation as one of the 10 most ecological buildings in the world.

Smart entrepreneurship + innovative, green technology = solutions that are profitable and sustainable.

In India, Narayan Hrudayalaya is a chain of "no frills" hospitals that will offer heart surgery at an astonishing price of $800. Compare this to the cost of open-heart surgery in the United States of over a quarter-million dollars and you begin to see how radical this solution is. How are they doing it? By using innovation and technology. The hospitals use prefabricated buildings, they strip them of all frills (including air-conditioning), and they then train visitors to help with post-operative care in order to reduce labor costs and make surgery affordable for the poor people who are in dire need of good-quality healthcare. As a result, Dr. Devi Shetty's "heart factory" in Bangalore does the highest number of cardiac operations in the world. Dr. Shetty also provides free treatment for the extremely poor, but believes, "Charity is not scalable. If you give anything free of cost, it is a matter of time before you run out of money, and people are not asking for anything free." The social entrepreneurship model of frugal innovation is sustainable and productive.

The Case of the Question Box

In India, one way we are bridging the digital divide and using technology to help people is via mobile phones. We are finding that mobile phones are just about the easiest way to gather and share information because they are cheap, easy to use, and do not require any specialized skill like reading, writing, or learning a potentially complicated Internet device. As such, we are seeing that the phones are an easy and affordable way to bring inclusiveness to the digital revolution that India, and the rest of the world, is witnessing.

See Figure 2.1 for an interesting example.

As you can see, people can ask questions at a metal, intercom-like box that is linked to a live operator. The operator in turn has direct access to the Internet. The box has a green power button, a microphone, and a speaker. The user pushes the button and is connected to the operator in real time. The Question Box uses a mobile phone inside the box with the extension of the buttons outside. Question Boxes bring the Internet information revolution to the masses via a simple phone call and, as such,

Push the green button to start (in local language). | Ask any questions! | An operator will look it up online. | And give you an immediate answer! | Push the red button when you are done.

Figure 2.1   The Question Box

allow users who are on the banks of the digital divide to cross the river and become part of the mainstream information revolution.

What do people ask of the Question Box? Questions cover a wide range of subjects, including cricket scores, paddy farming advice, codes to download songs on their mobiles, homework questions, university exam results, train schedules, commodity prices, and where to get a personal loan.

The Question Box is just the tip of the proverbial iceberg when it comes to using technology and frugal entrepreneurship to make the world a better, and smaller, place. In Africa, there is the One Laptop Per Child (OLPC) project, providing the poor with $100 computers. Nicholas Negroponte, the founder of the MIT Media Lab and co-inventor of OLPC, says, "Laptops, as we know them, are a luxury. Education is not. At $100, this is about learning and exploring, not giving kids costly tools and toys. Almost anything, from healthcare to food to birth control, can be addressed well, if not best, through education." He further points out, "The deeper divides are unequivocally proportional to education. Peace will never happen as long as there is poverty. Poverty can only be eliminated through education." The digital divide, though, can be bridged through inclusive participation, frugal innovation methods, education of the masses, and creation of a long-term plan. An empowered society is more economically stable and supports a humane lifestyle.

The Bottom Line

The world of the twenty-first century will need and see continued technological innovation—industrial innovation, e-innovation, frugal innovation, and more—because it is technological innovation that has always pushed us forward. The Edisons and the Eastmans gave way to the Jobses and the Zuckerbergs, and someday soon, the Zuckerbergs will give way to some other new incredible technological entrepreneur that no one has ever heard of.

That is the nature, the power, and the promise, of the technology entrepreneur.

■ ■ ■

Nikhil Agarwal is President of Cambridge Global Partners (CGP) and a researcher at the University of Edinburgh. Prior, he was Professor of Management and founder Director of Europe Asia Business School. Dr. Agarwal has founded businesses and advised firms on strategic matters in the past 17 years of his career. He has worked with global multinationals like Cadbury's, FIC, and Zensar (RPG Group). He has lectured at leading universities like Virginia Tech, the University of Bradford, the University of Edinburgh, and the University of Cambridge in visiting capacity.

His interviews and work has been extensively covered in international media including HBR, *Forbes*, CNN Money, BBC Radio, and the *New York Times*, to name a few. He has served on many international think-tanks and holds leadership positions in global organizations. He is serving as high-level-advisor to the United Nations Global Alliance on ICT & Development (UNGAID); is an international advisory board member at the World Entrepreneurship Forum, and a board member at the Open Mind Foundation.

Explorers of the New World

CHAPTER 3

Entrepreneurs: The New Global Adventurers

Dr. Colin Jones

Dr. Colin Jones, a seasoned entrepreneur, also coordinates the Entrepreneurship program at the University of Tasmania (Australia) and is the Senior Lecturer in Entrepreneurship at the university.

> Security is mostly a superstition. . . . Life is either a daring adventure, or nothing.
>
> —Helen Keller

*J*ust *as the global reach and experience of entrepreneurship is changing and growing in this new millennium, so too are the entrepreneurs who are making it happen. Whereas entrepreneurs—generally speaking—used to come from Western capitalistic democracies who created businesses that solved a local market need, that trend is also changing—radically, and for the better. Today, you are just as likely to see an entrepreneur emerge from an African valley as from the Silicon Valley.*

As entrepreneurship continues its march across the globe, it is inspiring a vast new generation of people to take risks and reach for the brass ring. Interestingly, and maybe not surprisingly, the businesses they are looking to start are as diverse as the regions they come from. Whether through a green start-up in South America, a social entrepreneurial experiment in Asia, or the latest tech innovation in the

United States, people everywhere are using entrepreneurship in new ways to solve new problems for new times.

Consider the Middle East.

In his excellent new book, Startup Rising: The Entrepreneurial Revolution Remaking the Middle East, *author Christopher Schroeder explains that there are plenty of reasons for innovation and entrepreneurship not to exist in the Arab world:*

> Added to political instability, the gap between the mega-wealthy and the desperately poor throughout the region remains shocking; education and literacy offer profound challenges. Corruption, high unemployment, heavy reliance on government largess, archaic and often indecipherable rules of law, and cultural resistance to investing beyond fixed assets are all daily realities.

Nevertheless, the exciting news is that Schroeder finds that Middle Eastern entrepreneurs actually have "hurricane force winds" at their backs, making an Arab entrepreneurial revolution a very real thing. These forces include:

1. *"Technology [that] offers an irreversible level of transparency, connectivity, and inexpensive access to capital and markets unprecedented only five years ago."*
2. *"Regional and global capital now more comfortable with political risk."*
3. *The fact that "changing market dynamics, growth, and opportunity in the Middle East were in motion well before the [Arab Spring]."*
4. *And finally, and maybe most importantly, the fact that "this new generation is hungry." The author quotes from an email he received from a young Jordanian: "Why should we except mediocre jobs in lumbering large companies or the government, assuming we can even find those?"*

The upshot of this is that there is an entrepreneurial revolution going on in the Middle East, just as there is across the rest of the planet—perhaps just a little more under the radar. But exist it does. As Schroeder says:

> These entrepreneurs come from every walk of Arab life. They are women and men, devoutly religious and culturally Islamic, college educated and self-taught, young and old and from

literally every country in the region. They are above all realistic about the odds against them, yet unfazed by the political and infrastructural barriers. . . . They are unleashing social and economic forces that will create the foundations of a new Middle East. These entrepreneurs are not naive. They expect setbacks. But they believe they are the right side of history.

"On the right side of history." You bet. It is this new breed of creative entrepreneur who is shaping, and will shape, the twenty-first century.

■ ■ ■

There has never been a time in the world's history when such lofty expectations have been placed on the entrepreneur by society. But with opportunity comes expectation. And as we have seen, today, what is expected of entrepreneurs is huge. Entrepreneurs, it would seem, are supposed to save struggling economies, renew dying towns, provide regions with economic prosperity, bring water to impoverished nations, and do it all before lunch.

Of course, some areas of the world are still more conducive to entrepreneurship than others, but that does not mean entrepreneurship is the domain of only a lucky few anymore—far from it. If you just consider the Middle Eastern entrepreneurs above, it is clear that almost anyone, anywhere can become entrepreneurial today.

What do we mean by "entrepreneurial"? For starters, of course, we mean the ability to start a business, but let me suggest that entrepreneurship now is more than just that. Instead, when I say "entrepreneurial," I am more broadly referring to the ability of individuals to *act differently* vis-à-vis the norms that surround them; that is, to be able to find new solutions to the challenges they see. While this may relate to business creation and/or reorientation, it may also equally apply to being an agent of change in a local community. But however you define it and however it might apply to you, the fact is, anyone today can become more entrepreneurial. In fact, in this world, you cannot afford *not* to be more entrepreneurial.

So what does it take to become an entrepreneur? It is easy to assume that those who do so are simply more motivated than those that don't. But that is just an easy answer. To assume that Microsoft's Bill Gates grew his business empire simply because he was more motivated ignores many pertinent facts, including that he grew up in the right time and place and gained immeasurably valuable experience writing computer code as a kid due to fortuitous access to new technology. Was he smart and motivated? Sure, but entrepreneurial success takes a whole lot more than that.

Among other things, it requires a sense of adventure.

The New Global Adventurers

The word *adventure* is often defined in terms of exciting and unusual experiences, complete with risks and uncertainty, and I am using it that way here on purpose. For, if nothing else, entrepreneurship is an adventure, complete with highs and lows, uncharted waters, dramatic breakthroughs, and, hopefully, plenty of smooth sailing.

Developed by Roy Heath at Princeton, there is a view out there of the entrepreneur as "the reasonable adventurer"—that is, someone who creates "opportunities for satisfaction." How does that sound to you? Whether it is your desire to create a great business that attracts venture-capital funding, a green business that solves an environmental need, or a community group that remedies a problem, doing so will require a sense of adventure and having (or developing) the various attributes required for creating opportunities for satisfaction. Wouldn't you like to be able to turn the mundane into a never-ending adventure through reorienting your view of the world you live in? To do so requires first and foremost *thinking* like an entrepreneur—like someone who appreciates adventure, but charts his or her course smartly.

Attributes of an Entrepreneur

Let me suggest that the idea of the entrepreneurial adventurer can be built around six specific attributes:

1. Vision
2. Emotional intelligence
3. Trusting your judgment
4. A tolerance of ambiguity
5. Being open-minded
6. A sense of humor

Let's now dig a bit deeper into each one of these qualities to see just how you too can cultivate these attributes and become the captain of your own entrepreneurial adventure. The first is that of *vision*.

Vision

Like the adventurers who discovered the New World, entrepreneurs often see something and believe something that others do not see and cannot believe. Entrepreneurs have a vision for a business, product, service, or innovation; they can see how it can make a difference; and they go about enlisting others' help in bringing that vision to fruition. It is no easy task, getting people to invest their money and reputation in your unproven, untried (ad)venture. Whether you are a man with a plan or Christopher Columbus, getting others to see what you see and invest in that dream requires supreme confidence in your ability to see far off into the distance.

Christopher Columbus began his quest to find a sponsor for his visionary expedition to Asia in the early 1480s. He believed that it would be faster to get to Asia by sailing west across the Atlantic Ocean instead of using the traditional route south around Africa. In the early 1480s, King John II of Portugal turned Columbus down. Undiscouraged, Columbus turned to Spain, where he met with, and was also turned down by, Queen Isabella I, in 1486. It was six years later, in 1492, and fully more than a decade after he began this part of his quest, that Columbus finally convinced Isabella and her husband, King Ferdinand V, to pay for his voyage. Funding—always an issue for adventurous entrepreneurs.

Visionaries of all sorts are able to see the mundane and imagine something much greater. As we go about our busy lives, each day we are constantly presented with scores of data and information, much of which we treat as fact. Fair enough. In an always-on world that is increasingly fast-paced, there is a temptation to keep moving on from bits to bits of information rather than to delve into the actual meaning of what is being presented. But to be a successful entrepreneurial adventurer, let me suggest that you need to be thoughtful and discerning. You need to be able to see what information is really important to consider and what is a tweet that needs to be ignored.

The entrepreneurial adventurer is therefore adept at alternating between involvement and detachment: being able to be both curious and critical, a believer and a skeptic. Consider Fred Smith's brainchild, FedEx. It required both the ability to see the extraordinary in the ordinary and the vision to carry that idea to fruition. While the general nature of postal delivery was not a major problem for society in the 1970s, Smith saw something that others did not. His insight and action introduced us to guaranteed overnight parcel delivery and forever changed the nature of business. Doing so required both a discerning eye *and* a clear vision of the future.

This is often a difficult concept for young entrepreneurs to grasp. Not all ideas are great ideas, and coming up with a great idea means not just moving from one piece of information to the next. How much time each day do you spend rethinking that which is taken for granted? Fred Smith looked at something as mundane as postal delivery and, because he gave it a fresh look, invented a whole new industry. Richard Branson looked at air travel and realized there was a better way. Henry Ford rethought ground transportation.

Entrepreneurs see the ordinary and envision the extraordinary.

In August of 1971 following a stint in the military, Fred Smith bought controlling interest in Arkansas Aviation Sales, located in Little Rock, Arkansas. While operating his new firm, Smith identified the tremendous difficulty in getting packages and other airfreight delivered within one to two days. This dilemma motivated him to do the necessary research for resolving the inefficient distribution system. Thus, the idea for Federal Express was born.

—FedEx.com

So take some time to rethink your assumptions, and daydream a bit. Write your ideas down. Read them to yourself. Share your best ones with a few trusted family members and friends. Your capacity to develop this first attribute depends upon your willingness to challenge your own current intellect. Dream, and dream big.

Emotional Intelligence

The second attribute of the entrepreneurial adventurer is that he or she is emotionally intelligent and understands the nature of close relationships. Being an entrepreneur means selling something to someone, right? Perhaps it is an idea or a service or product, but whatever it is, you need to enlist, enroll, and get others invested in your dreams and aspirations. How do you do that? The basic answer is that you must make connections with people, forge bonds, and appreciate how other people think and feel. That emotional intelligence is what enables you to create rapport with people and thereby form a great team. And it is the great team that wins championships.

To help foster this idea of emotional intelligence and the importance of teamwork in entrepreneurship, I focus explicitly on group work to force my students to listen to others and to look at situations from others' perspectives. When we develop strong friendships, we expose ourselves to a process of discovering that which we don't yet realize about others. As an educator, I try to create the conditions for such close friendships to blossom. Without a doubt, those students who take advantage of these conditions develop the confidence to act more entrepreneurially.

Trusting Your Judgment

To what extent do you base your life decisions upon external expectations instead of trusting your own personal judgment? Entrepreneurs lurk in the shadows of conformity waiting for the right moment to turn everything upside down, and as such, they necessarily trust their own judgment more than the status quo or prevailing norms.

Indeed, entrepreneurial adventurers are not dissuaded by dissention—just the opposite, in fact. Being surrounded by diverse opinions usually provides an entrepreneur with the opportunity to listen to and appreciate different points of view. To think and rethink. To be wrong. Ultimately, diverse opinions forcefully shared foster confidence in whatever decisions the entrepreneur finally makes.

I think you've got to create a culture in which dissent is valued. And there's probably a lot of ways to set that tone. Certainly you can tell if you've got a culture of dissent when you walk into a company. People can figure out very quickly whether dissent is encouraged or whether it's actually something that's not welcome.

—David Sacks, CEO of Yammer

We have now covered half of the attributes of the adventurer—the prototypical individual capable of entrepreneurial behavior and action. Take stock and evaluate yourself based on these attributes. What we are looking for is an individual whose ability to see through the ordinary fosters visionary, creative solutions. Someone with a willingness to challenge conventional facts while nurturing loyalty through emotional intelligence and personal connections.

Is this you?

Tolerance of Ambiguity

The one certain thing in the life of an entrepreneur is that nothing is for certain. You give up your job and steady paycheck for a life of ambiguity and uncertainty. The great philosopher John Dewey once stated, "Life is interruptions and recoveries." Most of life's interruptions are unplanned, and not all are easily overcome. The entrepreneurial adventurer gets that; he or she knows that life cannot be organized into simple black and white categories. Ambiguity rules the day.

Imagine, if you will, J. K. Rowling receiving rejection after rejection for her story of a young wizard named Harry. Certainly she might have concluded that this situation was very black and white. Yet Rowling also knew she had created something wholly unique, even if no one seemed to agree with her. She had a vision, trusted her judgment, and knew that there were shades of gray where others could only see yes or no, acceptance or rejection. (See, it's all coming together!) So she kept on. While it is doubtful that Rowling found this situation enjoyable, many entrepreneurs thrive on such uncertainty—they know that is where the juice is. Put another way, a visionary like Rowling can tolerate ambiguity because she knows that that (pardon the pun) is where the magic is.

So how well do you cope with not knowing? As an entrepreneur, you don't know a lot of things: You don't know if your idea will fly, you don't know if you will get funded, you don't know where customers will come from, you don't know what the competition will do—and that's just the beginning. Are you, as former U.S. Secretary of Defense Donald Rumsfeld famously suggested, capable of discovering the "unknown unknowns"? Doing so requires faith and trust. When we can trust an environment within which we are expected to make our way forward in the dark, metaphorically speaking, we develop a greater tolerance for ambiguity. But when we lack trust, when we revert to the safety of the known knowns, results become unextraordinary.

> There are known knowns; there are things we know that we know. There are known unknowns; that is to say, there are things that we now know we don't know. But there are also unknown unknowns—there are things we do not know we don't know.
>
> —Donald Rumsfeld, February 12, 2002

However, my experience with thousands of entrepreneurship students is that everyone can develop an increased ability to cope with ambiguity. Given that entrepreneurs seek to create that which does not yet exist, this is clearly an important entrepreneurial attribute.

Being Open-Minded

While I place equal importance on each attribute above and consider each one germane to the development of the entrepreneurial adventurer, I must admit a soft spot for this attribute. The reason is that whenever I have an idea or concept to share with my students, I always do so hoping they will be open-minded enough to connect it to their own lives. I hope they will develop an *uncommon interest in the commonplace.*

Open-mindedness—seeing something uncommon in the commonplace—can lead to extraordinary entrepreneurial breakthroughs. For example, one day, George de Mestral took a walk in the woods and ended up with scores of annoying little burrs in his socks. Instead of simply picking them out, as most of us would have done, de Mestral was curious: Why did the burrs cling to his socks? So he put one of the burrs under his new microscope and saw that it was made up of thousands of tiny hooks. Those hooks in turn caught the little loops that made up his sock. Ten years later, that exploration of the commonplace led to de Mestral's invention of . . . Velcro.

Again, the issue of being able to slow down and find fascination in the raw elements of everyday life emerges. Entrepreneurial adventurers not only envision amazing new things, they also remake the mundane and make it new again.

A Sense of Humor

Success in your entrepreneurial adventure certainly requires that you have a sense of humor: after all, sometimes, if you don't laugh you would cry. More importantly, humor:

- Makes employees and customers happier
- Connotes a confidence that others like
- Reminds you not to take it too seriously

According to research done by Chris Robert, Associate Professor of Management at the University of Missouri–Columbia, humor is key to a successful workplace and, by extension, to an entrepreneurial adventure. As discussed in *BusinessWeek* (November 5, 2007):

> The use of humor, and the ability to produce and make humor, is associated with intelligence and creativity, two things highly valued in workplaces. More important, the link between humor and positive emotions seems strong, which is intuitive, and there's also a strong correlation between positive emotions and workplace performance.

The upshot is that a sense of humor "can help promote a happy, productive workplace."

Sir Richard Branson tells a story about the importance of maintaining a sense of humor in business. Faced with the constant theft of salt and pepper shakers from Virgin Atlantic airplanes, Branson decided, "if you can't beat 'em, join 'em." So he had the phrase "Pinched from Virgin Atlantic" engraved on all of the shakers, thereby turning a negative into a funny little joke, as well as a great marketing ploy.

So there you go, my entrepreneurial adventuring friend. Does this sound like you? Are these six attributes behaviors that you have or could develop? More importantly, can you see the obvious relationship between these attributes, when taken together, and the way in which they will enable you to set sail on a successful entrepreneurial adventure? I hope so!

The Adventurer as Entrepreneur

These six attributes are just the starting place, the spot where you can discern whether you too can be an entrepreneurial adventurer. They are necessary because the world is continually evolving into a place where those who can cope with, and adapt to, this ever-changing, fast-moving, interconnected world of ambiguity will outperform those who cannot.

My ideal entrepreneur doesn't necessarily create large corporations or float IPOs (although some will); they might also simply create change in and around their communities, or start fine small businesses. Whatever the case, they have a vision of something better and find ways to challenge the status quo—in their own lives and in the world around them. They work well with others, allowing their outlook to be reshaped by gaining a better understanding of other points of view. They trust their judgment and use their experience to guide them through uncertain times. Perhaps most importantly, they see diamonds where others see dust, maintaining a fascination in that which others ignore. (Added bonus: They also make great dinner companions and tend to indulge in any opportunity to share happiness.)

At a time when the world is continually shrinking, entrepreneurship is expanding and opportunities abound. Accordingly, joining the ranks of the entrepreneurial adventurer is becoming an ever more attractive option for many. To succeed in this adventure, you will need an internal compass pointing you in the right direction, and you will have to trust that compass. You will also need mad skills, a good plan, and a dash of luck. To begin, to head off on your entrepreneurial adventure, you simply must be brave and willing to take a risk and sail off into lands unknown.

May the wind be at your back.

■ ■ ■

 **Dr. Colin Jones** has spent a lifetime being an entrepreneur, helping others to become entre-preneurial, and thinking about the process of entre-preneurship. Recently his attention has turned to understanding the hidden factors that influence busi-ness survival.

Dr. Jones coordinates the Entrepreneurship program at the Univer-sity of Tasmania (Australia) and is the Senior Lecturer in Entrepreneur-ship at the university. Prior to entering academia, Dr. Jones had extensive experience starting up and operating a range of service-related businesses. He has been recognized nationally and internationally for his research, teaching, and learning achievements. Dr. Jones has published more than 60 peer-reviewed journal and conference papers and recently published his first book, titled *Teaching Entrepreneurship to Undergraduates*.

CHAPTER 4

Going Green: Business as an Agent of Change

Thais Corral, in collaboration with Jarrod Russell and Daniele Cesano

Thais Corral, a social innovator and entrepreneur, has been a leader in the global movement for sustainable development for the last 25 years. She is the cofounder of the internationally recognized Women's Environment and Development Organization (WEDO).

> The message . . . [to] the business community is, there need not be any conflict between the environment and the economy. We will find the way not only to reconcile [those], but to find new profits and new opportunities as we do the right thing.
> —Former U.S. Vice-President Al Gore

*W*e *have all heard the terms by now: Sustainable development. Green business. Eco-friendly. Environmentally safe. But what do these things mean, really? Is it in fact possible to create businesses that are not only profitable but have a green conscience as well? The short answer is yes; in fact, not only is it possible, it is necessary for the sustainability of both business and the planet. Because the fact is, we cannot go on much longer the way we have been going. Something has to give. The good news is that, as we have seen throughout this book, entrepreneurship is malleable and entrepreneurs are creative. If anyone can figure out how to marry business and the environment, and make both prosper at the same time, it is the members of Planet Entrepreneur.*

■ ■ ■

The Seeds of Change

At the onset of the 1980s, Lester Brown, founder of the Worldwatch Institute, introduced us to the word *sustainability*. He defined a sustainable community as one that was capable of satisfying its own needs without undermining opportunities for future generations. Years later, the Brundtland Report,[1] under the auspices of the United Nations (UN), used the same idea to introduce the concept of sustainable development, "meeting the needs of the present without compromising the ability of future generations to meet their own needs." The report contains within it two key concepts:

1. The concept of needs, in particular, the essential needs of the world's poor, to which overriding priority should be given
2. The idea of limitations, imposed by the state of technology and social organization on the environment's ability to meet present and future needs[2]

The expression *sustainable development* became popular during the 1990s. At the beginning of the decade, the UN organized one of its biggest international conferences, the United Nations Conference on Environment and Development. It was hosted in Rio de Janeiro, Brazil, and is now commonly referred to as the Rio Conference. This conference represented a breakthrough in how government agencies, private entities, and civil society interact. For the first time in the UN's history, these seemingly disparate sectors of society were invited to build a platform of action together, called Agenda 21.

Agenda 21 offered a policy for sustainable development and allowed previously excluded sectors to participate, strategize, and collaborate within this important global debate. With its 48 chapters, Agenda 21 addresses significant environmental and social challenges that we will have to face together, globally, in this generation and the next. But it represents much more than a 48-chapter white paper. Agenda 21 is an innovative socio-environmental contract defining our shared challenge and articulating the role that women, unions, local authorities, national

---

[1] www.un-documents.net/wced-ocf.htm.

[2] Ibid.

governments, international institutions, nongovernmental organizations (NGOs), the private sector, the scientific community, indigenous communities, and youth have in contributing to the solution: the transition to sustainable development, to a sustainable future.

During the 1990s, governments and international institutions were the primary drivers of the sustainable development agenda. Unfortunately, their efforts largely failed to meet high global expectations born of Agenda 21 in the coupling of social, economic, and environmental benefits. There was, however, a silver lining. Ironically, out of this underwhelming global effort led by behemoth governments and institutions, there emerged focused local initiatives led by individuals, people, and groups from civil society.

The local dimension of these efforts enjoyed unprecedented visibility and support during the inaugural Rio Conference. Local Agenda 21 became the most popular achievement of Agenda 21. For example, hundreds of cities around the world reorganized their local city councils to create opportunities for people of diverse backgrounds, cultures, and streams of knowledge to collaborate. By envisioning a better world together, the logic went, these groups could more effectively delegate and share responsibilities to create such a world.

The Rio Conference, also known as the Earth Summit, was an extraordinary affair. One hundred seventy-two governments participated, including 108 heads of state, and over 24,000 NGOs were in attendance. Several milestone agreements came out of the summit, including the predecessor of the Kyoto Protocol. Additionally, the Convention on Biological Diversity was first signed at the Rio Conference. A dozen cities around the world were also commended for their environmental programs.

Another great outcome of Agenda 21 was the rise of women as agents for and protagonists of sustainability. WEDO (www.wedo.org), cofounded by Thais Corral, is an organization that supports this global effort. WEDO catalyzed an international women's movement for sustainability. Not only did this movement help transform the nomenclature of official UN documents, it also introduced a new culture in the community of institutions working in the field of sustainability.

Such institutions typically are founded in the northwestern part of the globe and predominantly advocate for environmental conservation in the Southern and Eastern Hemispheres, and yet even so, they give little consideration to how to actually motivate and improve these local communities they are so concerned about. Lots of theory. Poverty and population growth were seen as abstract problems rather than part of a complex ecosystem in peril that required equally complex, innovative solutions. Women were best suited to bring the human and family-level dimension into sustainability. They have enriched the debate so that *equity* and *equality* have become commonplace words in negotiation rooms and explicit topics in sustainable action plans.

Discussions sparked ever-evolving questions. Protection of the environment and satisfaction of human needs are now converging as mutual calls for action. Questions and conversations about these goals have expanded over the past couple of decades, including the debate between the North and South; the distribution of resources, power, and hierarchies; and competing worldviews. The best outcomes from this evolution of cooperation for sustainable development could be summarized as:

- Emerging multistakeholder, multicultural dialogues and partnerships
- Balancing of top-down and bottom-up agendas with respect to problem identification and implementation strategies
- Understanding that in order to develop effective solutions, these partnerships must look to nature and cultures as the teachers of environmental coexistence and innovation

> We are not going to be able to operate our Spaceship Earth successfully nor for much longer unless we see it as a whole spaceship and our fate as common. It has to be everybody or nobody.
>
> —Buckminster Fuller

Now, in the second decade of the twenty-first century, a new global perception has emerged: Humanity is unquestionably degrading the planet and things need to change. Thus, doing nothing is no longer an option. Anthropogenic change and apathy cannot be allowed to cohabitate if sustainable development is truly a global priority. The belief that economic growth in a finite world will, alone, solve the problems of poverty is simply not credible anymore. How can it be if it undermines the very ecosystems upon which we all depend? Furthermore, beyond purely environmental concerns, the fact that the wealth of the 200 richest people in the world exceeds the combined annual income of the world's 2.5 billion poorest people is a poignant example of the problem of wealth disparity that we also face.[3]

That business is the driving force in our society is an important indication of where this paradigm has to shift. But true innovation requires thinking differently about the responsibilities businesses have to their consumers, host communities, and countries. A variety of businesses and organizations have already come to this realization. Some have been acting on this understanding for years while others are working hard to catch up. Yet, many organizations still remain in a state of inaction amidst this challenging backdrop of social, economic, technological, and environmental flux.

It is hard to manage chaos, no doubt about it. However, more and more, businesses in every sector are incorporating sustainability as a central component of their strategic planning and brand. They accept that they must do so if they wish to survive and thrive in the tumultuous times ahead. Understanding how sustainability influences CEO- and board-level decision-making is vital. Furthermore, as Gaylord Nelson, United States Senator and founder of Earth Day put it: "The economy is a wholly owned subsidiary of the environment, not the other way around."[4] Similarly, there can be no healthy economy without a stable and vibrant social order. As Jeffrey Sachs indicates in his book *The End of Poverty*, business cannot thrive in environments where there is corruption, the absence of the rule of law, and hunger.[5]

---

[3] *State of the World 2012: Moving Towards Sustainable Prosperity.* The Worldwatch Institute (www.worldwatch.org).

[4] Walter Link, Thais Corral, and Mark Gerzon, *Leadership Is Global* (San Francisco, CA: Global Leadership Network, 2006).

[5] Jeffrey Sachs, *The End of Poverty—Economic Possibilities for Our Time* (New York: Penguin Press, 2005).

The Emergence of the Green Economy Paradigm

The 2012 Rio Conference (aka Rio + 20) focused on the green economy, showing that the only way to shift priorities is to integrate sustainability into business. This move is distinguished from prior environmental paradigms in that it develops mechanisms and metrics to value the use and abuse of natural resources in corporate and national accounting. The premise of this shift is the possibility of a full-cost accounting regime—including more comprehensive pricing mechanisms to account for negative externalities. The concept of a green economy does not replace sustainable development but rather asserts that sustainability depends on getting the economy right. It presents a new economic paradigm: one in which material wealth is not delivered at the expense of the environment, natural resources, and society.

In pursuit of sustainability, a green economy strives for low-carbon, resource efficient, and socially inclusive development. Income and employment are driven by public and private investments that reduce carbon emissions and pollution, enhance energy and resource efficiency, and prevent the loss of biodiversity and ecosystem services.

For governments, this would include leveling the playing field for greener products by phasing out antiquated subsidies, reforming policies and providing new incentives, strengthening market infrastructure and market-based mechanisms, redirecting public investment, and greening public procurement. For the private sector, this would involve understanding and sizing opportunities represented by green economy transitions across a number of key sectors, and responding to policy reforms and price signals through higher levels of financing and investment.

The United Nations Environment Program defines a green economy as one that results in "improved human well-being and social equity, while significantly reducing environmental risks and ecological scarcities."[6] Rio + 20—the international conference assembled by the UN in June 2012 to celebrate the 20th anniversary of the Rio

---

[6] UNEP 2010.

Conference—helped the concept of the green economy gain strength, largely fueled by the perception that sustainability politics could not be implemented efficiently. The climate of the economic crisis further promoted a shift towards economic valuation of resources, establishing economic rationale at the foreground of approaches to environmentalism.

During the past two decades, capital was poured into property, fossil fuels, and structured financial assets with embedded derivatives. Comparatively little was invested in renewable energy, energy efficiency, public transportation, sustainable agriculture, ecosystem and biodiversity protection, and land and water conservation. Existing policies and market incentives have contributed to this problem of capital misallocation by allowing businesses to run up significant, largely unaccounted-for, and unchecked social and environmental externalities.

How do we change? In the book *The Necessary Revolution*, Peter Senge and others say that the Iron Age didn't end because we ran out of iron.[7] Similarly, the Industrial Age isn't ending because of the decline in opportunities for further industrial expansion. "It is ending because individuals, companies, and governments are coming to the realization that its side effects are unsustainable." In the face of such immense challenges and uncertainty, there is, not surprisingly, resistance. Not a few people and institutions are working to maintain the status quo, promoting policies and implementing strategies that support business-as-usual (BAU) operations.

Fortunately, there is an emerging community of business and social entrepreneurs who are stepping forward to create flourishing new businesses, networks, and organizations. These frontrunners are shaping the economy of the future by embracing green, with both vision and faith. What exactly is a *green business*? According to BusinessDictionary.com, "A green business is a business functioning in a capacity where no negative impact is made on the local or global environment, the community, or the economy. A green business will also engage in forward-thinking policies for environmental concerns and policies affecting human rights."

---

[7] Peter Senge, Bryan Smith, Nina Krushwitz, Joe Laur, and Sara Schley, *The Necessary Revolution—How Individuals and Organizations Are Working Together to Create a Sustainable World* (New York: Random House, 2008).

What many entrepreneurs are seeing increasingly is that there are ample business opportunities in the green world. As Inc.com says, "Sustainability isn't just about venture-backed tech firms and big manufacturers" (www.inc.com/green). In its second annual eco-business special report, Inc. examines some of the top green enterprises and how they are transforming business—and the world:

Prometheus Energy: Traps methane gas from landfills and "converts it into liquefied natural gas to power buses and other vehicles."

Seahorse Power: Makes garbage cans using solar-powered trash compactors, thereby increasing capacity while reducing the number of picksups required by municipal clients.

Southwest Windpower: Another company that sees green in green energy, the business sells small wind turbines—to residential customers.

Burgerville: A hamburger chain that not only sells organic fast food, but runs on wind power, uses cooking oil waste to create clean-burning biodiesel, and demands that all its paper products be biodegradable.

Clif Bars: Produces energy bars made of organic ingredients. Offsets fossil fuel usage with a wind farm. Delivery trucks are run on biodiesel. Eliminated shrink-wrap packaging.

IceStone: Manufactures countertops, flooring, and wall coverings from recycled glass and concrete.

Extengine Transport Systems: Takes old diesel-powered trucks and construction equipment and retrofits them with an engine system that reduces emissions by up to 90 percent.

Verdant Power: Submerges turbines in waterways to "convert the power of natural currents into household electricity."

So the stage is set. In today's interconnected world, the challenges are global and the pace of change is rapid. Progressive-thinking individuals and organizations from around the world are experimenting with new ways to live and work together. They strive to transform social and environmental challenges into business opportunities for the benefit of not only themselves and their families, but also entire communities. They seek pragmatic, yet inspired solutions, moving beyond heroic individualism to collective intelligence and collaborative action.

New Business Models for a New Era

There exists today a set of new business entities called *social enterprises*, or *benefit corporations*. At the center of their business models are mechanisms that generate wealth while discovering solutions for unmet social and/or environmental needs. These enterprises define profit not only by accounting for the revenue they generate, but also by integrating their socio-environmental mission statement and by-laws as the bedrock of their strategic planning, driving a new perspective of how to generate and measure their profits. Therefore, the social and environmental benefits they create are included in their accounting and performance metrics. Put simply, by staying true to mission statements and by-laws, benefit corporations do much more than maximize investor returns, yet they tend to perform very well on this front, too. This is a new concept that is spreading very rapidly.

As of today, there are 765 benefit corporations certified in 27 countries across 60 industries. Several new organizations are being created to support existing enterprises such as Ethical Market Place (www.ethicalmarketplace .com) and the B Lab (www.bcorporation.net). Two of sustainable development's biggest proponents, Sir Richard Branson and Jochen Zeitz, are developing a new network of leaders called the B Team to accelerate the transition to a world of thriving B Corporations.[8] By developing entirely new organizations designed to restructure the relationship between private, public, and nongovernment institutions, building truly collaborative ventures, we can reconnect marginalized communities and restore damaged ecosystems. The potential benefits of these new ventures are enormous, as they transform the way in which communities articulate their human, natural, and financial resources.

SIR RICHARD BRANSON LAUNCHES THE B TEAM TO REVOLUTIONIZE BUSINESS GOALS

It is time for business to be a "force for good," says Sir Richard Branson in describing his new venture, The B Team. The B Team is his new global non-profit that promises to champion "a new way of doing business that prioritizes people and planet alongside profit—a 'Plan B' for businesses the world over."

(continued)

---

[8] www.heraldonline.com/2013/06/13/4942297/richard-branson-and-jochen-zeitz.html.

> (*continued*)
>
> "Plan A—where companies have been driven by the profit motive alone—is no longer acceptable." Co-founder Jochen Zeitz, former CEO of Puma, explains that while business is integral to society, it has "also created most of the negative environmental challenges of this century. The B Team will help to catalyze a shift away from the existing short-term, unsustainable mindset, towards the long-term interest of people, the planet and the wider economy."
>
> From SustainableBusiness.com News, June 2013.

One key characteristic of said ventures, on an ever globalizing planet, is that they operate in focused territories, deepening their integration and increasing the probability of success. We will present an example of one of these collaborative ventures called Adapta Sertão (which was created, in part, by the authors of this chapter).

Sustainable Development in Action

Poverty is endemic in Brazil's semi-arid region, the Sertão. With about 20 million people, the region accounts for 50 percent of Brazil's most impoverished citizens. Local economies are based on inefficient agriculture practices. Such production inefficiencies, coupled with an increasingly erratic climate, are the main drives of regional poverty.

Highly variable rainfall and recurrent droughts typify the Sertão's climate—phenomena that are expected to worsen due to climate change.[9] As a result, major reductions in household crop yields are the new normal in the region, threatening food security. The Food and Agriculture Organization of the United Nations (FAO) estimates global food production must double by 2050 to prevent mass hunger, with developing and emerging economies expected to provide growth in consumption and production.[10] The problem is widespread, but therein lies the opportunity for widespread collaboration.

In response to such concerning trends, Adapta Sertão was started in 2004 by REDEH, a social and environmental nonprofit based in Rio de Janeiro. REDEH believed that the obstacles undermining the Sertão's

[9] UN IPCC.

[10] www.fao.org.

communities represented untapped commercial solutions and business opportunities. A green business solution was possible.

They started by identifying the obstacles to improving crop yields:

• Inadequate retail channels for irrigation technologies
• Lack of financial mechanisms to catalyze innovation
• Lack of technical assistance for farmers
• Deforestation

Within these obstacles were the seeds to solutions, becoming Adapta Sertão's core objectives:

• Disseminate efficient irrigation technologies to farmers
• Commercialize farmers' products
• Restore the local biome

So, as you can see, Adapta Sertão was born out of necessity, an example of how—despite severe conditions—it is possible to create business opportunities that benefit socio-environmental regeneration.

Adapta Sertão: Improving Small–Farmer Livelihoods through Green Entrepreneurship

Value creation processes need to be reorganized in order to create economic capital while developing social capital and preserving natural capital.
—Jost Hamschmidt

Adapta Sertão began in Pintadas, Bahia, in the Sertão. It is a small town surrounded by subsistence farmers. Times are tough given the troubling drought that descended in late 2010. Drought is not abnormal in the Sertão, but climate change research shows the region's average daily annual temperature increased by 1.75 degrees Celsius and annual precipitation fell by 30 percent over the last 50 years. Furthermore, with only 16 percent of the original and local biome (caatinga) intact, deforestation undermines the local ecosystem and climate.

What to do?

Through a collaborative partnership between civil society, private enterprises, public institutions, and underserved communities, a strategy was envisioned. At the center of this innovative effort is Adapta Sertão.

Adapta Sertão's success starts with a simple approach: Build solid partnerships with local farmer associations (i.e. cooperatives). Each cooperative is responsible for its respective local technology distribution network. For example, irrigation systems reduce manual labor and water consumption. Drought resistant crops and balanced feedstock improve crop yields and livestock productivity. Small-scale desalinization systems using brackish water are proving commercially viable. For financing, Adapta Sertão empowers local credit cooperatives to manage revolving funds. Another important element is human capital. Adapta Sertão works with agricultural professionals throughout Brazil to develop toolkits, helping farmers grow organic crops, recuperate soil quality, and diversify animal feed. Program toolkits and best-practices information are available online (www.adaptasertao.net).

To get farmers' products to market, Adapta Sertão is developing its own brand. In 2011, for example, by collaborating with local manufacturers and regional supermarket chains, Adapta Sertão began helping farmers commercialize their organic products. A new processing plant is already in operation, profitable, and proving that there are local, renewable assets just waiting to be developed for commercial use. By identifying a number of local fruit trees that are resilient to drought and produce fruits all year, Adapta Sertão is helping the Sertão go local. Exotic trees like umbu, seriguela, and passion fruit trees produce fruits that can be processed, frozen, and sold. Herein lies another opportunity beyond just conservation; these green businesses are also financially sustainable.

By modernizing local agricultural production systems, Adapta Sertão is reducing the rural exodus to urban areas, helping to alleviate pressure on favelas (traditionally poor, marginalized urban communities in Brazil). By promoting healthier communities that produce and buy local foods, Adapta Sertão is redirecting the allocation of public resources.

New Metrics to Assess Success

So, as we can see, the traditional business paradigm is rapidly evolving, raising questions about the effectiveness of ubiquitous metrics such as GDP, which continues to dominate the way in which the wealth of countries is measured. This metric accounts for financial activities but neglects to account for a wide range of other indicators for a society's overall wellbeing. For example, GDP makes the plight of indebted

European countries look much worse than it really is. "Looking at their well-educated workforces, modern infrastructures and productive land and ecosystems—all count for zero in GDP," says Hazel Henderson. For the last 30 years, Henderson has been advocating for new indicators of quality of life to orient the financial and industrial markets. As one of the pioneers of the global movement Beyond GDP, Henderson emphasizes that love, caring, nurturing, sharing, and cooperation are still predominant in our human family, which she calls "the love economy."

Coined in 1972 by Bhutan's fourth Dragon King, Jigme Singye Wangchuck, the phrase "Gross National Happiness" is a term used in Bhutan to build and measure their economy, based on the country's Buddhist values and, yes, the happiness of the populace. The phrase now serves as the underlying basis for Bhutan's five-year planning process and all policies that guide the economic development of the country.

Looking Forward

The new realities mentioned in this chapter pose serious challenges to us all, threatening especially the way business entrepreneurs understand systems. The awareness of growing interdependence shows that it is more important than ever to learn how to expand the boundaries of attention and concern regarding the ways in which businesses operate. Many natural resources such as forests, fish stocks, water, and topsoil are declining because businesses and communities follow strategies that maximize short-term production without understanding the larger system and perceiving that they are consuming resources more rapidly than they can be regenerated. At a certain point, expanding boundaries and facing deeper problems opens peoples eyes to totally new opportunities. Alcoa and Coca Cola are two examples of big companies that have embraced the rethinking of water usage. Just by looking into the way they were using water, they became a positive force for water management globally.

The trend is that businesses are working together on green energy, carbon reductions, and other sound sustainability strategies, such as the certification of fish and forest products. The need for public and private partnerships and collaboration among companies has been established. We just need to understand how to get better at it, and how to educate and gain the attention of many more entrepreneurs. Quickly.

■ ■ ■

 **Thais Corral,** a social innovator and entrepreneur, joined the World Entrepreneurship Forum in 2010. She has been a leader in the global movement for sustainable development for the past 25 years. She is the cofounder of internationally recognized organizations such as WEDO and REDEH (www.redeh.org .br). She is also the initiator of social enterprises such as Adapta Sertão (www.adaptasertao.net) and SINAL do Vale (www.sinaldovale.net). She holds a master's degree from the Harvard Kennedy School of Government and lives in Brazil.

Daniele Cesano is Technical Coordinator of Adapta Sertão, a social venture that promotes rural development in northeast Brazil, and Managing Director of Onda Verde Consulting, Rio de Janeiro, Brazil. He holds a PhD in Earth and Water Resources from the Royal Technical Institute of Technology, Stockholm, Sweden.

Jarrod Russell received a B.A. and a master's degree from the University of California, San Diego (UCSD), focusing on corporate responsibility and energy economics. He has worked at the Carter Center in Bolivia, the Baja Project in Mexico, CB Richard Ellis and Adapta Sertão in Brazil, and San Diego State University in Australia. Currently, he is the director of business development for an international nutrition company called Nutrition Stn.

CHAPTER 5

Social Entrepreneurship and the End of Charity

Tony Meloto

Tony Meloto is the founder of Gawad Kalinga, a nongovernmental organization building more than 2,000 sustainable communities in slum areas in the Philippines and East Asia.

One of the newest figures to emerge on the world stage in recent years is the social entrepreneur. This is usually someone who burns with desire to make a positive social impact on the world, but believes that the best way of doing it is, as the saying goes, not by giving poor people a fish and feeding them for a day, but by teaching them to fish, in hopes of feeding them for a lifetime. I have come to know several social entrepreneurs in recent years, and most combine a business school brain with a social worker's heart.

— Thomas L. Friedman, *New York Times* columnist

*O*f all of the changes that have emerged in the last decade in the quick-moving, vastly changing world of entrepreneurship, social entrepreneurship has to be near the top of the list. Social entrepreneurship is a new way of solving old problems, of remedying perceived social inequities and societal issues.

What is the old way? Usually, when someone felt compelled to right a wrong, he or she might start a nonprofit or a foundation or an NGO, solicit funds from wealthy donors, write grant proposal upon grant proposal . . . and then do it all again the next year. Pleading for charity and money, no matter how noble the cause, can quickly and easily cause burnout—both among those asking and, equally, among the askees.

That is why social entrepreneurship is so revolutionary. It combines the best of both worlds. By taking a play out of the entrepreneur's playbook and applying entrepreneurial principles and strategies to a social cause, the social entrepreneur seeks to create self-sustaining entities that rely far less on the kindness of strangers and far more upon self-reliance.

■ ■ ■

My Life as a Filipino Social Entrepreneur

Although my simple motivation when I started my journey as a social entrepreneur in 1995 was to find hope for my four children who were growing up in a country that was in darkness due to deepening poverty and corruption, I now find myself with the challenge of working for inclusive growth through social entrepreneurship at this time when the Philippines is suddenly one of the fastest rising economies in Asia. In three years, the country has fought corruption and instituted the economic reforms and bold tax measures that gave the Philippines its first investment grade status from Standard & Poor's and Fitch—and a GDP of 7.8 percent that was the highest in Asia in the first quarter of 2013. This kind of rapid rise to the top creates a problem of greater social inequity if benefits remain in the hands of the small elite minority that controls the economy.

I have spent nearly two decades working for poverty eradication with a nonprofit global movement called Gawad Kalinga, which means literally "to give care." Our mission is to help end poverty in the Philippines. We have had many successes due to the generosity of the human heart when inspired to sacrifice for the greater good as well as a greater consciousness among the young created by social entrepreneurship. Like many impoverished countries, the Philippines has both great resources and great needs. As a social entrepreneur, our challenge in the beginning was to design a replicable template of sustainable communities that addressed fundamental human needs. These included:

• Land for the landless
• Home for the homeless
• Food for the hungry
• Water for the thirsty

How did we do this? We created shared value by tapping the resources and expertise of the more privileged to develop the skills and talent of the less fortunate. Showing that this kind of model works has caused more communities to be built, not only by our workers and volunteers, but also by national and local government units and local communities.

After building a prototype intentional community for 2,000 families in Bagong Silang, the biggest slum in the Philippines north of Manila, we have been able to replicate the model in 2,000 villages nationwide and four countries abroad, including Indonesia, Cambodia, Papua New Guinea, and Australia. Through this work we are starting the process of transforming the lives of our beneficiaries, neighboring communities, volunteers, and interns through our programs for shelter, health, education and values formation, entrepreneurship and livelihood, and environment, with a specific focus on climate change, renewable energy, and food security.

Poverty in our country being massive, our response could not be small, and finding solutions had to be done collectively. To achieve this we had to have a big, noble, and doable dream; otherwise it would not attract those in business, government, and civil society to join us and create a bandwagon for nation building. But join us they did. Top public officials from presidents to mayors, corporate CEOs and heads of universities, and Filipino diaspora groups abroad gave support and made Gawad Kalinga a popular choice in the work of community transformation and poverty eradication.

Our model has taken on many forms:

- A group of five professional women who are active volunteers of Gawad Kalinga formed a social enterprise of their own called GKonomics that helps develop, fund, produce, and market the products of 200 communities and provides livelihood for over 3,000 mothers. They are supported by corporations and volunteers in creating a nationwide network for training, marketing, and distribution.
- Human Nature was started as a social enterprise for natural, organic personal care and cosmetic products from the kitchen of my eldest daughter, Anna, and her younger sister, Camille. With the entrepreneurial experience of Anna's British husband Dylan Wilk, in four years, they turned the company into a nationwide social business

whose products were distributed by 70,000 dealers with 26 branch stores and retailed in leading supermarkets and malls. They provide livelihood to farmers in 20 rural communities, paying them higher-than-market prices and using profit to build schools, expand their branch, and improve their production facilities. They also provide jobs to former scavengers in eight Gawad Kalinga (GK) villages around the Payatas dumpsite, giving them nearly double the legal wage, social security, and healthcare. For its massive impact, Human Nature was chosen as Social Entrepreneur of the Year by Ernst & Young and Schwab in 2012.

- Another former GK volunteer now turned successful social entrepreneur is Reese Fernandez-Ruiz. She collaborated with top fashion designers to provide jobs and dividends to mothers living near dumpsites by converting trash to cash. The high-end bags of her social enterprise, *Rags to Riches*, can be found in top stores in the Philippines and abroad, worn by fashionable ladies as the Hermes and Gucci in the world of the new elite—those with the most who create the best from the least.

Our original plan was simply to turn ugly shanties into brightly colored homes complete with sanitary toilets, clean water, and landscaped gardens, thus transforming troubled neighborhoods into peaceful communities. But the vision just keeps growing, giving birth to bigger and better ideas and many additional ancillary benefits.

Corporations are getting in on the game too. For instance, not a few corporations have discovered that involving their employees in volunteer work in our communities has improved the morale of employees and enhanced productivity. Through this effort, we have transformed slums and helped improve the living conditions of workers. Since our organization's inception, over 500 corporations have built communities with us by providing funds to build homes, schools, and livelihood programs with the help of their employees.

The Age of the Social Entrepreneur

But do not think that social entrepreneurship is just an activity that takes place in poor countries. Often it does, sometimes it does not. For example, the Food Recovery Network (FRN) in the U.S. works to recover surplus perishable food that would otherwise go to waste from university campuses. The group picks up the excess food and delivers it to homeless shelters, food banks, and other nonprofits in the surrounding communities.

Or consider this story from *Bloomberg Businessweek* (June 7, 2013):

Asad Ali is a 20-year-old medical student at the University of Oslo in Norway. His motivation for becoming a doctor is to help people. He says it's the same desire that drove him to enroll in the Global Social Entrepreneurship Institute at the Kelley School of Business.

The program is meant to help Ali and 19 other college-aged students from Europe gain business skills to help alleviate poverty, foster economic development, and support communities in their homelands. The Department of State's Bureau of Educational and Cultural Affairs, which is sponsoring the institute, and the Fulbright Program, which offers grants for Americans to study abroad and for international students to study in the United States, chose the participants, who come from across Europe, including Greece, Spain, and Portugal.

"These are the rule breakers of tomorrow," says the managing director of the Institute for International Business at the Kelley School.

The rule breakers of tomorrow. Indeed.

As Thomas Friedman says, the social entrepreneur is someone with a brain for business and a heart for people. Social entrepreneurship is a transformational new way to solve societal problems. All at once it is simultaneously changing the nature of:

- Charity
- Poverty
- Economies
- Entrepreneurship itself

Radical Change: The Mood of the Times

It is the need for change that has given birth to social entrepreneurship. Social entrepreneurs are people like:

- Patrick Struebi, founder of Fairtrasa (Fairtrade South America). Fairtrasa helps small-scale farmers in third-world countries improve their lives by providing them with "technical support and access to international markets. The company works to ensure that farmers are paid fair prices for their goods, which can often be up to 10 times higher than local market prices, and helps them increase their yields to become self-sufficient and grow beyond subsistence level" (ABCNews.com, December 21, 2012).
- Melissa Kushner, the World Entrepreneurship Forum's Young Entrepreneur for the World in 2012, who created an amazing program called Goods for Good (GFG) in 2006. GFG gets American companies with excess goods to donate these provisions to needy African communities. To date, GFG has distributed 1.4 million pens, 116,200 shoes, and 23,000 school uniforms and garments to over 70,000 orphans and vulnerable children in Africa. Adding to this, GFG has launched small on-site businesses in these African communities designed to "generate income and fund orphan care programs for education, health, and nutrition. These businesses, which include chicken farms, agriculture enterprises, and tailoring co-ops, create jobs, stimulate the local economy, and ensure the children have every opportunity to thrive" (Goods4Good.org).

The goal of the social entrepreneur is to create economies that promote justice and fairness and refuse to leave anyone behind. Social entrepreneurship is about utilizing business and professional tools to find solutions to social problems, either as nonprofits or as for-profits, and is a work that has always been associated with philanthropy since it puts great value on compassion and doing good for others. Organizations that fit this mold include groups like Habitat for Humanity, World Vision, Oxfam, and Save the Children. These big charity organizations have originated in wealthier countries like the United States and the United Kingdom, born out of the compassion and generosity of those who have more in life toward the less fortunate and suffering in less developed areas.

The reason there has been a shift to social entrepreneurship is that many of these big nonprofit groups have found it difficult to sustain their operations using a traditional charity model that necessitates competition for limited or diminishing philanthropic funds. Donor fatigue, too, is a real thing. The challenge has been in finding creative strategies for sustained giving.

Enter social entrepreneurship. The magic of social entrepreneurship is that it is in fact sustainable. No longer must charities compete for limited funds or hit up donors again and again. Instead, social entrepreneurship offers the hope of creating entities that supply their own funding while still accomplishing the charitable goal.

The rise in global attention to social entrepreneurship as a solution to social problems began with the phenomenal success of Grameen Bank and the charisma of Nobel Peace Prize winner Muhammad Yunus. His bank was the first to give microloans to millions of poor clients in Bangladesh and India in support of new microbusinesses. The average Grameen Bank loan is less than $100.

Yet, whereas many charity organizations began in countries classified as first-world, today we are seeing many social entrepreneurs originating from the emerging economies of Brazil, India, Bangladesh, and the Philippines, where the challenge is raising the bottom of the pyramid without destroying ecology or seeing government, big business, the rich, and the landed as adversary or foe. Because it is about inclusive growth, social entrepreneurship is also, necessarily, about peaceful change. It is about working with multinational corporations in this age of globalization to grow local brands using indigenous ingredients and talent and not seeing each other as competitors. Instead, with this new model, creating local and sustainable businesses becomes an investment in expanding the market base and doing business in a more productive and sustainable way.

Global Proof

Given that the purpose of social entrepreneurship is to address local social issues, it follows then that social entrepreneurs must respond to the needs and opportunities of the countries from which they come. Thus, for instance:

The focus is on the environment in Brazil, where many entrepreneurs are passionate about the preservation of the Amazon and its entire ecosystem. Not only do they seek to guard the culture of the tribal communities, but they are also making great strides to protect indigenous flora and fauna.

Additionally, according to the Stanford Social Innovation Review (July 28, 2011), "The overall Brazilian economy, led by the agricultural, manufacturing, and mining sectors, is booming. Over the past ten years, Brazil has averaged 3.2 percent annual GDP growth. [While] the benefits of economic growth are being felt throughout the country, more than 40 million Brazilians are still living below the poverty line, and Brazilian entrepreneurs are emerging to address the needs of this marginalized population. Throughout the country, entrepreneurs are exploring market-based solutions to poverty challenges, including access to affordable housing, healthcare services, and information technology."

In Africa, many international celebrities have demonstrated their passion for making a difference with direct action. For example, Oprah Winfrey has used her huge personal resources and massive popularity to get public support to open a modern school in Johannesburg, South Africa, for gifted girls regardless of religion, race, or ethnic background. The Oprah Winfrey Leadership Academy for Girls seeks solutions through education to address a lack of opportunity for women in African societies.

In India, social entrepreneurship is often geared towards empowerment of women and technological innovations to address poverty. Social entrepreneurs are using a variety of business models to do everything from funding women-led microbusinesses to burning dung to heat villages.

In Bangladesh, the focus is also on women, with microenterprise as the means toward self-sufficiency. This being the home of Grameen Bank, it has also enticed big global corporations to come and incubate their concept of social business, like the French company Dannon, which set up an enterprise producing yogurt to improve health and create livelihood for the poor.

Our own program in the Philippines is a good example of how social entrepreneurship works, and can work, throughout the world. In our case, to create a bigger platform whereby we could attract more volunteers and donors and thereby help more people, we did not go for a project mentality with a timeline for entry and exit. Instead, we went for a nation-building movement strategy with a 21-year development timeline. Our idea was to create an open platform for massive volunteerism and heroism, where measures are both quantitative and qualitative, with a clear end-goal of helping end poverty in our country by 2024. We know that our goal is a giant one, but our commitment to its success is, too.

In Jakarta social entrepreneurship is being used to help the poorest of the poor. Businessman Arif Rachmat, along with his family and friends from the corporate world, raised funds to buy land, hire community organizers, and conduct values formation and skills training to residents of dumpsites and slum areas. The idea is to use entrepreneurship to hire and train the poor, thereby helping them get out of the cycle of poverty with honor and dignity and through patriotism, hard work, and sacrifice. And not by depending on foreign aid.

> Social entrepreneurship is the place where charity, sustainability, entrepreneurship, idealism, and realism intersect.

So, what is a social entrepreneur? Social entrepreneurs are the bridge of the poverty gap. They use the best corporate expertise and practices to produce quality products, enterprises, and businesses that both do good, and do well. Social entrepreneurship is a multifaceted diamond that shines as it is held up at different angles and to different light.

Challenges of Social Entrepreneurship

The challenge for social entrepreneurs in most third-world countries is twofold. First, there is the question of how to help grow the local economy and protect the environment by raising a new generation of wealth creators at home, rather than just job-seekers abroad. And secondly, how to become producers of home-grown, ethical, quality made-at-home brands using local raw materials and skills, instead of having people consume expensive foreign brands or cheap and even dangerous contaminated imported goods.

Other challenges include:

1. How to use the social entrepreneurship platform to attract and support business, finance, management, science, and design graduates from top universities, instead of losing them to better paying opportunities overseas. Emerging countries need the best and the brightest to stay in-country and develop for-profit social enterprises that will be pro-poor, pro-environment, and pro-country.
2. How to get big business to help social entrepreneurs incubate and grow their social enterprises and see them as wise investments. Social entrepreneurs need corporations to understand that doing good for the poor and for nature makes good business sense for everyone.
3. How to gain government support for social entrepreneurs through investment, tax and subsidy incentives, farm-to-market roads, irrigation and post-harvest facilities, training, and technology in partnership with farmers and skilled workers.
4. How to create a convergence of the public and private, the rich and poor, the city entrepreneur and rural farmer, so as to become co-collaborators in creating shared abundance for the greater good.
5. How to get the children of the rich in cities to come to understand that the land and the poor in rural areas can be income generators.

How Does One Become a Social Entrepreneur?

Despite these obstacles, it should be (hopefully!) clear that social entrepreneurship is not only a huge, emerging trend, but a satisfying career choice as well. Here are some fundamental facts:

1. **There is no age limit to being a social entrepreneur.** You might be a student going for an internship in a social enterprise in your country or abroad. Or you can be a new graduate who will plunge into social entrepreneurship even without corporate experience. You might even be a corporate executive who creates a social business on weekends with family or friends, at home or in a nearby poor

community. Social entrepreneurs can even begin late, as many retirees start social enterprises as an exciting second career.

Most of all, and most likely, you can be an ordinary citizen who sees a social problem in your community and just wants to do something about it.

Which one are you?

2. **There are many types and approaches to being a social entrepreneur.** You can start a nonprofit or a for-profit. You can do it alone or with family and friends. You can start a social enterprise or you can join an existing one. You can do it full-time or part-time.

3. **Government should be a friend of development and social entrepreneurs.** Avail yourself of the best training and support that government and other agencies can offer. Study the laws and regulations, get the necessary permits and licenses, and obey the rules. Create a platform for public/private partnership. Learn to deal with politicians without being partisan or compromising your integrity. Support worthy government efforts where you are needed and can have the most impact.

> To gain access to government funding sources, we use a strategy we call "counterparting." We build homes, schools, clinics, and livelihood centers using private funds from our corporate and civil-society partners. In return, the government "counterparts" with roads, water systems, and other public infrastructure; provides programs for livelihood, education, health, and environment; gives training and equipment; and hires consultants and project teams to work with us.

4. **To become a successful social entrepreneur, grow the heart and mind.** As you can see, being a social entrepreneur is a special calling, one that is challenging for sure, but incredibly satisfying as well. To live the life of a social entrepreneur, let me suggest that you remember the "5 Cs":
   ○ **Character:** Live with honor, make good your word, endure, stand up after falling, finish what you start. Discard bad habits, walk your talk. Start to work when others are asleep. Work for value, not money. Have a building philosophy, not a funding mentality.

- **Compassion:** Know the power of love and patience, relate with kindness, understand forgiveness, build the greater good through caring and sharing, grow market by making the weak strong, turn liability into asset by restoring human dignity.
- **Courage:** Do not fear failure, challenge the impossible, get out of your comfort zone, smile at those who laugh at your idea, encourage others who are faint-hearted. Eat stress for breakfast. Fight fiercely with kindness. Do more good when bad things are done to you. Victory is in the journey of those who fight for good and never give up what is right.
- **Competence:** Use the genius of the mind to fight with the goodness of the heart. Give the best to the least—use the best expertise, the best technology to bring the bottom of the pyramid up. Charity is about pity purchase, whilst social entrepreneurship is about nurturing excellence and efficiency from those we pity. Partner with people who have the knowledge and expertise that you do not have.
- **Commitment:** Do not quit—never even think of quitting.

■ ■ ■

Born near squalid living conditions in the Philippines, **Antonio Meloto** (also known as "Tito Tony") graduated from university in 1971 with a Bachelor of Arts in Economics. Afterwards, he became a manager at Procter & Gamble and eventually became a successful entrepreneur.

It was while working in Australia that he felt the powerful call to start the work with the poor by creating a youth development program for gang members. Since it began in 1995, the program has now evolved to become Gawad Kalinga, a global movement that builds integrated, holistic, and sustainable communities in slum areas. Gawad Kalinga is now being implemented in almost 2,000 communities in the Philippines and in other developing countries such as Indonesia, Cambodia, and Papua New Guinea. Believing that poverty is not so much about the scarcity of resources than it is about the loss of human dignity, the organization tries to bridge the gap between the rich and the poor and between government and the private sector.

CHAPTER 6

Empowering Women and Minority Entrepreneurship

Jeannie E. Javelosa

Jeannie E. Javelosa is a writer and author, strategic brand communications specialist, and a social entrepreneur. She advocates around the world for culture, sustainability, and women's economic empowerment.

Countries and companies will thrive if women are educated and engaged as fundamental pillars of the economy.
—Klaus Schwab, Founder and Executive Chairman
of the World Economic Forum

*J*ust *as social entrepreneurs are shaking up traditional models of philanthropy and sustainability, so too are women and other so-called "minorities" changing the shape of business, entrepreneurship, and indeed whole economies. The change is vast and rapid and obvious everywhere you look:*

- *New economic centers are migrating from West to East*
- *Ventures that combine people and the planet are becoming more prevalent*
- *Business models that require diversity in their supply chains challenge the norm are on the rise*

And if entrepreneurs generally are out to use and shape these events, female entrepreneurs specifically are out not only to do that, but to transform society at the deepest levels. Stats and data abound to support the conclusion that when women are economically empowered, money is recycled back into businesses and toward the health, education, and well-being of the family. Women in leadership positions, both in the corporate world as well as in policy-making, are creating a future that is more humane and compassionate, and societies that are more collaborative and sustainable.

So what we want to do in this chapter is share the news (both good and bad) about female and minority entrepreneurship generally, and then give women and minorities specifically some tips on starting their own entrepreneurial venture.

■ ■ ■

Female Entrepreneurs

From a large-scale perspective, female entrepreneurs encompass approximately one-third of all entrepreneurs worldwide. But even so, many are not prosperous, especially the millions who live in Asia and Africa. These women hail from the informal microbusiness sector, where we find the least productivity and the least amount of resources. Educational choices, traditional views and stereotypes about women, and greater time restrictions due to household and family responsibilities add to the long list of challenges these women entrepreneurs encounter. Indeed, many of these women still face old-style gender-role issues. Entrepreneurship in many places in the world is still considered a masculine field, and it still proves difficult for women to surpass these conventional views.

Although women are not minorities per se, they have been in the minority when it comes to starting businesses that make it big. Women have simply not been able to scale businesses compared with their male counterparts. There are many reasons for this:

- A lack of, and difficulty in, accessing finance and capital
- Limited technical and scientific knowledge
- Limited or sometimes even a complete lack of business, management, and marketing skills and training
- Inadequate market access

- Restricted control over resources
- Inability to own land, and thus a lack of collateral for business loans, and then, as a result, almost no access to formal finance
- Lack of access to information, equipment, suppliers, and buyers
- Fewer business networks and role models

Women entrepreneurs in many places in Africa, as well as in some Middle Eastern and Asian countries, where strong fundamental cultural views prevail, often find it even more difficult to get credit as they may need to obtain their husband's consent or signature first.

Compared with their male counterparts, who can access capital far more easily, women are therefore often forced into the world of microcredit and microloans. The problem with that, with women being unable to access real finance, is that they are then unable to create growth businesses that are scalable. Many women then are stuck in a cycle of small business, small credit, small business.

In the developing world, patterns of women entrepreneurship are different than those in the developed world. Growth there is generally slow too, and the female-owned businesses that do succeed are usually smaller, less profitable businesses. In wealthier economies, while women entrepreneurs tend to be older, educated, and just as likely to create innovative products, their growth expectations are half that of men.

Yet, while there are clearly inherent cultural and structural barriers to female entrepreneurship in the developing world, there is also much progress being made. For starters, global policy groups are now focusing on how to help women increase their productivity. The work is to understand the barriers that prevent women from creating businesses that can scale, and why they have yet to fully participate in some specialized entrepreneurial activities, especially in science and technology. Additionally, the global entrepreneurial tide lifts all boats, not just male boats. Women the world over are in the process of reclaiming, balancing, and redefining their own power. Many are finding the inner power to break limitations created by their own minds due to culture and gender biases, and second, they are gaining external power to effect entrepreneurial economic success. Women entrepreneurs are therefore, increasingly and despite the challenges, becoming a global force to reckon with.

A timeline of global directions from policy-creating agencies dedicated to supporting women's economic empowerment and entrepreneurial activities:

- In 1998, the Asia-Pacific Economic Cooperation (APEC) held its First Ministerial Meeting on Women in Manila, Philippines, which brought the "woman agenda" into focused discussion with first specific steps to reinforce the important role of women in economic development and integrate them into mainstream.
- In 2002, in Guadalajara, Mexico, the Second Ministerial Meeting on Women continued gender integration.
- In 2006, the Global Gender Gap Report series was launched. The United Nations (UN) and World Bank Group, consisting of academics, policymakers, economists, and business leaders, stated that a country's competitiveness depends on the degree to which it educates girls and women and leverages untapped female talent.
- In 2010, the Policy Partnership on Women and the Economy (PPWE) was formed to create better collaboration between the public and private sectors, and to better mainstream gender across APEC economic growth strategies.
- In 2010 UN Women was created by the UN, bringing all women-led agencies and programs under one umbrella.
- In 2011 the APEC Women and the Economy Summit in San Francisco adopted the San Francisco Declaration that identified significant milestones in convening the public and private sector to discuss the significance of women's economic potential. Key global platforms were born from this summit.
- In 2012 in St. Petersburg, Russia, the APEC Women and the Economy Forum built on the San Francisco Declaration and focused on women entrepreneurship, science, and technology, and the importance of work-life balance.

Minority Entrepreneurship

World economies all see the potential to foster growth and job opportunities of another important pool: minority entrepreneurs. Under this general heading, we include migrant and ethnic, indigenous or cultural minorities, the young, seniors, the disabled, and the LGBT (lesbian, gay, bisexual, transsexual) community. Businesses owned by these groups have a significant impact and their entrepreneurship can and does significantly influence national economies.

Europe and the United States take the lead in supporting and promoting migrant and ethnic minority entrepreneurs and work to help these groups overcome difficulties that might prevent them from starting and growing businesses. In the United States, minorities own 15.1 percent of all businesses, with a majority of the businesses owned by Hispanics, Asians, Blacks, and American Indians. In the United Kingdom, Asian and African/Caribbean entrepreneurial groups predominate. (However, with the shifting economic winds blowing from the West to the East, you never know—Westerners may soon find themselves minorities of the economies of China, India, and Asia.)

Minority entrepreneurs face similar challenges as female entrepreneurs, but unique to the former are:

- Language and cultural barriers
- Family and community labor that is both a vital resource and a hindrance to the businesses
- An overconcentration in low-entry threshold activities where the scope for breakouts or diversification into mainstream markets may be limited
- Overly catering and relying on their own ethnic markets instead of branching into other markets

Young people in particular are turning to entrepreneurship in increasing numbers for many of the same reasons as women and minorities: to be their own boss, to hopefully make more money, for freedom, for creativity, and to deal with unemployment and as a buffer against economic slowdowns. While formal and informal educational systems, councils, summits, grants, and training programs are mushrooming globally to support them, the young often find themselves disadvantaged, especially when they attempt to embark on entrepreneurial endeavors.

The good news is that here, too, there is more help than ever available. For the most part, this is due to technology and the Internet. Once land-locked to their locale, the young now have instant access to the entire world. They see young Chinese making millions and they want to do it too. That they are able to use the Internet to learn, network, share, create e-businesses, and market those businesses makes that more than a pipe dream, it makes entrepreneurship very viable.

In the United States, 81 percent of high school dropouts say they would have stayed in school had the subject matter been more relevant. Seventy percent of all high school students say they would like to start their own business someday. And 75 percent of prison inmates are high school dropouts. Lesson: Teach entrepreneurship in high school, and both the dropout and crime rates should decrease.

Senior or older entrepreneurs are often classified under "economically nonactive groups" who later in life may decide to start businesses. They do so for their own reasons: to increase their pensionable income, to be able to sustain the lifestyle they are used to, to provide an opportunity to pursue their own personal interests, to make life "beyond retirement" more enjoyable, to fight boredom, and to further their own sense of identity.

The good news is that whether out of necessity or desire, older entrepreneurs have several competitive advantages. They have experience and are knowledgeable in their field. They have networks. They may even have savings. And here again, with technological breakthroughs allowing them to work from home, entry into the market as entrepreneurs is more doable for the elderly than ever.

Do they have their own challenges? Of course:

- Many senior women have not been able to amass a pool of financial resources
- They may have limited social capital (i.e., a lack of network and business connections)
- They may have physical limitations
- They may face societal preconceived notions

For all of these special breeds of entrepreneurs, there are increasing ways to launch and sustain the adventure. There are boot camps and trainings both online and offline, financial and credit support, and global policies and local legislation to help and strengthen the practice and participation of these entrepreneurial segments. Networks of these individuals are generally smaller and less diverse than those of their male, mainstream counterparts, but they are there and there is strength in numbers.

How can we help these entrepreneurs? If you are male, consider mentoring a woman, or a minority, or hiring and training a disabled person. Do business with female and minority entrepreneurs. If you are a woman and in a position of authority or decision making, work with women and minority entrepreneurs and entrepreneurial networks. Together, in collaboration, we can think big and succeed in breaking through comfort zones, geographical locations, and mind limitations that prevent us from succeeding and getting ahead.

What Does It Take to Live the Dream?

I began as an artist with no knowledge of business, management, or finances, but the entrepreneurial spirit was always present in me. I dreamt big even as I stumbled and learned entrepreneurship along the way. When my business partners and I launched our ECHOstore Sustainable Lifestyle, we stayed within our niche specialty market carrying the "ECHO" DNA or value systems that support environment, community, hope, and organization (hence "ECHO"). We sell green, fair trade products in store-café-markets, made and produced by marginalized communities to help livelihood, alleviate poverty, and green the earth.

Our ECHOsi Foundation (an acronym for "Empowering Communities with Hope and Opportunities through Sustainable Initiatives") focuses on helping marginalized and micro-entrepreneurs, giving them access to markets, and bringing small and medium enterprises and corporate business into the whole value chain and up to the global market. We own the Great Women Program and Brand, which is about women helping women up the value chain. The gap we stepped into was the loop of sustainability within the value-adding development-production-supply-market chain that addresses social and environmental issues, through a women-led social enterprise.

Three decades later, I find myself sitting on corporate boards, leading two NGOs, and owning and running a number of successful businesses aside from ECHOstore. Today, I address groups of women in international conferences and policy creation meetings, sharing the ideas of female economic empowerment. I am lucky that here in Asia, in this small Philippine archipelago of 7,100 islands that I call home, we have had two women presidents, have one of the most progressive women empowerment laws, and have a Magna Carta for Women.

And yet, while women like me are becoming increasingly more entrepreneurial, gender evaporates when we look at what constitutes the entrepreneurial spirit. So let me ask you: Do you notice any of these qualities in yourself:

• Do you enjoy birthing ideas, innovating, and giving life to a new venture?
• Do you like the excitement of creating new ventures?
• Do you demonstrate initiative and independence?
• Would you rather work for yourself than others?
• Is there a restlessness in your soul to "rebel" and improve the status quo, a longing to seize opportunities that can help improve the existing order and create new jobs and better services?
• Do you like swimming against the tide?
• Do you like working long hours and can you live with stress?

If you answer "yes" to the majority of these questions, then read on to begin living your dream.

The Path of the Entrepreneur

To be a successful entrepreneur is to also be aware of business cycles. Someone nurturing a start-up has different needs and goals from someone managing a large staff and demanding customers. From a start-up (either as a young entrepreneur marked by opportunities, or one born out of necessity after starting a family, raising children, and wanting to return to the workspace) to the scaling-up phase of creating a complete organizational, production, or corporate cycle, I have observed some patterns:

• Years 1–3 are the start-up phase marked by the exciting, passion-filled, structure-creating, brand positioning, market-opening period.

- Year 4 marks the need to show profitability and can be the first pivot of the cycle.
- Years 5–7 are used for steading the structural and professional organization of the business.
- Year 7 is where the business rocks, with the challenge to change or innovate products and services, shift directions or markets, and to perhaps bring other partners or professionals in to bring business to a new level. This is repeated in every 7-cycle (7, 14, 21, 28, 35, etc.). These are the real pivot cycles that force growth, expanding, restructuring, rebranding, or reorganization.

Passion

With that overview, the question then is, how do you start? Usually, it is best to begin with your passion. What is it you enjoy doing? And what comes naturally? The answer to these questions is where you will find potentials for business ideas. Passion alone will not carry you and your business to success, but passion is the fuel that will carry you through the shifts, turns, and challenges of running your business.

Passion also works to your advantage when you can identify whether you are pulled to being an entrepreneur by *necessity* (meaning, you may need to augment your family income to try to meet expenses of children growing up), or *opportunity* (meaning, you see a market need and look to fill it). Necessity will keep you working at your business even if you may not totally enjoy it, while opportunity will give you new possibilities that foster excitement and passion. Either way, passion is what fuels the fire and will be both necessary and needed.

Invest in Yourself

To succeed as an entrepreneur—whether you are male or female, disabled or abled, black or white or blue—requires that you present yourself professionally, intelligently, and appropriately. Your personal brand is what people perceive about you. It is what they say and how they feel about anything related to you and what you are doing. While other self-help management techniques focus on self-*improvement*, personal branding suggests instead that success comes from self-*packaging*. Dress for success. Look and act and be professional. Know your desired brand and put it out there. And then do it some more.

> Create a list of business trainings that you can attend. These will help you to break your boundaries. Do one or two a year. While institutions and groups offer such trainings in person, there are also many less expensive choices available online:
>
> - Take a course on finances and how to write your business plan
> - Learn how to speak in public—great for business presentations
> - Take a class on marketing, personal branding, and sales
> - Attend a talk on personal investment
> - Subscribe to an entrepreneurial, business, market intelligence, or trends magazine or e-newsletter
> - Watch out for business associations that offer forum discussions on things related to your industry

Risk Taking

Conventional thinkers categorize "risk behavior" as negative. But this trait is essential to entrepreneurs. Multiple studies show that women are more adverse to risk than men. Yes, there will always be the chance the business will fail. But the desire for gain and the unwillingness to accept defeat is what should drive you forward. Risk taking should be smart and calculated. Study all impacts to your business from all angles, then find the courage to take the risk for expansion or change. As a woman or minority, it is this taking of a risk and leaping into the unknown that can allow you to overcome cultural and physical impediments and help you get to the next level.

Understand Your Financials

I cannot stress enough that you need to know your numbers. I learned everything the hard, painful way by losing money, so I would like to double underline this section. Your enterprise can be scaled for success if you understand the nitty-gritty of margins, profit levels, taxes, and so on If you don't have it in you, you need to find a financial consultant who can help you build a solid financial model. Your financial story will also be the basis for bank loans and capital infusion by angel funders, venture capitalists, and investors. Know your numbers.

Know Your Market

Equally importantly, you must know your market because this is where entrepreneurial ideas come from. The market will tell you what it needs. And because the market is constantly shifting and becoming more segmented, listening to it carefully is critical. With technology thrown into the equation, and with everyone wanting to personalize their needs, a key strategy is to look for the gap in the market and try to see how your product or service can address it. Add that to the puzzle and you may just have yourself a winner.

Social Capital

One advantage women have is that they seem to intuitively understand interpersonal relationships better than men. And, as they say, business is all about relationships, so the lesson is clear: Here is one place where women have a distinct advantage over men vis-à-vis entrepreneurship.

One golden rule I have followed is that when I meet people, I actually think of what I can give or share with them. It is a bit untraditional in that most people think of what they can get from a new contact, but really, there is the underlying universal truth that in giving with honesty and integrity, you will receive something back. I continually see how this works for me. Building trust-based relationships that turn into friendships that evolve into strong business partnerships helps me broker effective relationships and build social capital.

Within these relationships you are building you will inevitably find a mentor: someone you sincerely trust and who can teach you things professionally, someone who inspires you. While he or she can be a friend, it helps if the mentor is someone in your professional field or similar industry. Or you can be the mentor and help budding entrepreneurs build business intelligence, find their voice, and face their own tough challenges.

Another thing you will find is that as your build your mentor–mentee relationship, your mentor's network will open to you. The power of networking will become clearer, and you will meet new contacts.

Social Media

Understanding, using, exploring and exploiting social media as an entrepreneur is key in today's business world. It will be worth your time to study and learn about them because navigating the online world is a necessity for relevance and success today. You can develop and strengthen your personal and company brand, build networks, obtain network intelligence, find mentors, and also learn from industry and business leaders. Use this space strategically. Learn to develop and post key messages that build your desired brand.

> Connect with the "connectors"—these are people who link others to many others. These people are the fulcrum of groups and they naturally have the gift of relating and connecting people.

Pivoting

Pivoting is the act of turning from one direction to another. It suggests movement. In small, entrepreneurial businesses, the need to pivot remains ever present. Learning from mistakes, dealing with an angry customer, seizing an opportunity—all require a quick pivot. Pivoting requires being nimble, armed with the confidence that in taking calculated risks, you are serving the market, your business, and your customers.

Collaborations

In the great balancing of the world economy from the West to East, from the style of profit-oriented businesses slowly transforming to inclusiveness and embracing social inequalities, we are getting a deeper understanding of the nature of this energy that drives the changes. These are obvious in the rise of women's involvement in nation-building and policy creation, in the boardrooms of corporations, in the small enterprises that steadily support livelihood, in the homes where the fulcrum of life emanates from a woman.

We see this too in the numerous women-led alliances sprouting up across the globe; the men who advocate with their own gender to support this balancing. We see how technology connects and enables the expansion of global entrepreneurial networks for the minority entrepreneurs highlighting the diversity in our world. Worthy to note is that business and civil society have joined together, helping develop systems and implementation of programs, especially in developing nations. Corporations look to supplier diversity as an inclusive initiative that links private businesses with minority-owned suppliers of goods and services.

The essence is this: Women and minorities are making the world a better, more prosperous place as equality, empowerment, and social justice are being propelled forward by our entrepreneurial enterprises.

■ ■ ■

Jeannie E. Javelosa is a writer and book author, strategic communications specialist and an entrepreneur. Jeannie graduated with a Masters of Fine Arts from the University of Pennsylvania and has worked for international culture-related projects in ASEAN and Europe. Her experience also includes business development consultancy for two companies between Asia Pacific (China-Hong Kong-Australia), Europe (France-Italy) and the United Arab Emirates.

Her entrepreneurial involvements include co-founding a 15-year-old communications agency called EON Stakeholder Relations Firm, the social enterprise ECHOstore Sustainable Lifestyle, and the EC-Art Management Company. She also runs the ECHOsi Foundation that runs development programs to support entrepreneurial activities through the supply-value chain. ECHOsi also runs and develops the The Great Women Development Platform and Brand.

Jeannie continues to be invited to speak internationally on issues of culture, gender, diversity, and sustainability in the ASEAN region, Netherlands and Paris in Europe, and Jordan in the Middle East. She also writes a regular column at the Philippine Star and blogs at the *Huffington Post*.

CHAPTER 7

Untapped Potential at the Base of the Pyramid

Jack Sim

Named a Time *magazine Hero of the Environment and a Schwab Foundation Social Entrepreneur of the Year, Jack Sim is also known as "Mr. Toilet" for his creation of the World Toilet Organization and his efforts to bring sanitation to the developing world.*

> If a values–driven approach to business can begin to redirect . . . power towards more constructive ends than the simple accumulation of wealth, the human race and Planet Earth will have a fighting chance.
>
> —Ben Cohen, *Values-Driven Business: How to Change the World, Make Money, and Have Fun*

The world's population has now exceeded 7 billion people. But, as we all know too well, the distribution of wealth is very uneven. Consider this amazing statistic: While 40 percent of people (3 billion) owns 95 percent of the world's money, the other 60 percent, fully 4 billion people, owns only 5 percent. These underclass 4 billion people make up what is known as "The Base of the Pyramid," or BOP.

It is no secret that the BOP presents the planet with major challenges—what is the best way to feed, clothe, house, and educate these people? Certainly that is a debate that has been going on for eons. But the interesting thing is that, from an entrepreneurial perspective, the Base of the Pyramid also offers an incredible opportunity. For starters, consider just how big this "market" is—4 billion potential customers. Entrepreneurship can also be used to help the BOP help themselves—"teach them how to fish" instead of just giving them fish, as has been the case. And we can create incentives to business to create solutions for housing, food, sanitation, etc.

What we are learning is that the Base of the Pyramid, these needy 4 billion people, are far better off being served by entrepreneurship than almost anything else. Consider the case of China: How did China verge on becoming the world's biggest economic power in just over a single generation? In no small measure it is because they (1) set loose the entrepreneurial spirit that was clearly dormant in the country, and (2) saw the potential of serving the BOP through entrepreneurship and capitalistic market-driven goods and services, instead of top-down, state-planned economic dictates. Of course it is true that dire poverty still exists in the Middle Kingdom, but it is equally if not more true that the greatest anti-poverty, entrepreneurial program in the history of mankind was China's decision to unleash the entrepreneur.

The lesson is, free aid does not really work for the long term. Consider Africa. Forty years ago, Africa's poverty rate was 10 percent of its population; today, after an estimated $2 trillion in Overseas Development Aid (ODA) given by developed countries, Africa's poverty rate is a staggering 80 percent. Why is that? Corrupt dictators, stolen aid, endless wars, and disrespect for the rule of law are of course major reasons. But consider this, too: Giving free food hurts indigenous farmers and damages their livelihood. Sending in free doctors may mean the local doctors have to leave the country to make a living. Giving people free fish means they never have to learn how to fish.

Now compare this to, say, Singapore. In 1965, Singapore was poorer than Cambodia. Yet it was transformed into one of the richest countries on earth, per capita, in one generation. How? By adopting a market-based paradigm. The speed of Singapore's growth from developing to developed status can be directly attributed to the country's embracing the spirit of enterprise as a core cultural value. Similarly, China, India, Brazil, and other countries that applied the lessons of entrepreneurship to their economies have seen similar amazing results.

■ ■ ■

Problems at the Top of the Pyramid, Too

While there are well-known and obvious problems at the 60 percent Base of the Pyramid, there are other, different, problems facing the 40 percent at the top. For instance, as computer software replaces manual labor and machine automation increases productivity growth, fewer first-world workers are needed. This trend looks set to grow. To make matters worse, a globalized marketplace means jobs are outsourced abroad to lower costs. In developed countries, jobless rates recently hit unprecedented levels.

It is estimated that 70 percent of all of today's jobs will not exist by 2030. It is more likely that machines and software will replace human's jobs than the other way around.

Poverty in these developed countries is also growing and consumption is shrinking while money is being pushed up to the top 1 percent of the world's population. Meanwhile, as bigger and stronger companies succeed, smaller ones face increased global competition in the race to sell to the rich and middle-class. Indeed, most products and services worldwide compete to serve only 3 billion people who are seen as attractive customers.

The 4 billion people at the Base of the Pyramid earn less than $10 a day, mostly less than $4 per day.

A New Equilibrium

But now, with the advent of the entrepreneurial world economy, companies are discovering that these people at the Base of the Pyramid—those who live in relative poverty—are actually the world's biggest socio-economic group of customers waiting to buy products and services. This vast, virtually untapped marketplace represents the greatest number of new customers in the world.

For example, the BOP is one of the fastest growing markets in the world for cell phones and financing. Although the BOP's incomes in current U.S. dollars are less than $3.35 a day in Brazil, $2.11 in China, $1.89 in Ghana, and $1.56 in India, their potential volume of consumption *cumulatively* adds up to an estimated $6 trillion global consumer market today.

Six trillion dollars.

The BOP needs everything from food, housing, water, sanitation, detergent, and clothes to energy, home appliances, healthcare, transportation, education, entertainment, and financial services. For the clever entrepreneur, this is certainly a market opportunity.

If this market is so juicy, how could it have been neglected for so long? Maybe you are thinking that it is not profitable. Au contraire! For starters, we have always been presented with only one image of the poor: the destitute. But the poor are far more diverse than that. Yes, the poor are the starving children we see on TV. They are the farmers, who are rich at harvest time and poor the rest of the time, the fishermen, who are rich in the morning and poor in the evening, the pedicab drivers, whose wages depend on the weather and festivities, the factory workers, servants, cottage industries like weavers, petty traders, craftsmen, and so on.

But while we know that something like a tsunami or some other sudden disaster requires our immediate assistance, the fact is, the poor will never achieve self-sustainability unless we help them help themselves through economic empowerment. We need to nurture and train people living at the BOP to become entrepreneurs so as to create jobs, generate profits, grow their economy, and deliver a better quality of life. Through our injection of initial investments to build their capacity to help themselves through market-based solutions, we can increase their income; create an efficient demand and supply mechanism inside their local economy; and deliver their basic needs faster, cheaper, better, and easier than if we send foreigners to hand out freebies.

The Poverty Penalty

A significant problem those at the BOP face is the so-called "poverty penalty." That is, surprisingly, that they don't pay *less* for goods and services, they generally pay *more*. And as such, strangely, the gross profit margin at the BOP is rather high, and so we say that the BOP market is actually quite dysfunctional. The poor pay these higher prices, a penalty as it were, for many reasons, but a main one is a lack of market infrastructure—things like roads, talent, distributors, warehousing, and logistics are all weak or nonexistent at the BOP. As a result, big corporations find it hard and expensive to serve and penetrate this marketplace. Additionally, a typical BOP order is very small and so, without volume sales, serving each tiny order can entail high operating overheads per dollar of sales. In addition, the modus operandi of the big corporation is not adapted to selling to the poor. You don't send a salesman in a jacket and tie to the BOP. It is just too expensive to do that.

Another reason why the poor often pay double the price paid by wealthier consumers is because they lack access to multiple suppliers. There is no competition to drive down prices, another aspect of the "poverty penalty." While we in the developed world get water relatively free from the tap and subsidized sewage systems, the poor have to buy water by the can and build their own sanitation treatment system or suffer the indignity of open defecation. Lack of sanitation, hygiene, water, and hand washing with soap also causes 2.5 million deaths from preventable diseases each year.

> Personal example: I recently interviewed an entrepreneur at a microfinance meeting in Mexico. She borrowed $1,000 at a whopping interest rate of 42 percent per annum. I asked her how she could make any profit with such high cost of capital. She told me she collects orders for shoes from her village, buys the shoes cheap from the city, and sells them at double her cost and thus earns a hefty profit from her customers. Even owing money at 42 percent, she makes a substantial profit, and if you multiply that by billions of people, you see why the poor stay poor.

So helping the BOP is not easy, but that is where the opportunity for the entrepreneur comes in. It will be the entrepreneurial mind that can figure out how to work within this informal distribution networks to deliver goods and services, and thereby reap the profit, from the BOP. Fortunately, there are already many social entrepreneurs available for partnership on the ground. Out of the 3,000 Ashoka Fellows in the world, easily half of them are serving the BOP, and these prequalified fellows are certainly ready partners for any investor, philanthropist, or corporation that is looking to enter the BOP.

In the world today, roughly 1.3 billion people live without electricity, 2.5 billion without proper sanitation, 750 million are without safe drinking water, 2.7 billion are unbanked, and more than 1 billion live in slums. These numbers are rapidly growing. It is estimated that by 2030, 2 billion people will live in slums, leaving the farms to find jobs in the cities. But this is why we need to create a vibrant and efficient marketplace to bring about a more equitable society for the BOP, one where true competition means lower prices and wider choices for the poor.

Learning Curve

Not surprisingly, then, especially where instantaneous global information moves freely, the opportunity to both help the poor and make money in the process is becoming ever more apparent. As such, the BOP has also recently attracted many impact investors. However, these investors are reporting that while money is not the problem, it is hard to find good projects to invest in. Why? The learning curve of how to design for the BOP has taught us many lessons that to be successful, products needs to be not just affordable, but socially acceptable too. For example:

- A "Lifestraw filter" might filter dirty water, but hardly anyone of sound mind would risk drinking dirty water through such a straw directly into their mouth. They need to see clean water coming out of the filter before they drink it.
- A rollable water container (the Q Drum) was not only too expensive, but it actually made little sense. The cost was such that it could not compete with the price of a pail of water on the head, and furthermore, where terrain is not flat, pulling a water container uphill is more difficult than carrying it on the head.

Additionally, to be successful, BOP products need to be aspirational as well as useful. In contrast with those products mentioned before, the mobile phone has taken the BOP marketplace by storm because it is affordable *and* also aspirational—giving the poor social status when they own one. To be successful, therefore, designers are learning that a deep understanding of the poor's social norms is important. So now, often, they are involving customers during the early design stages and working backwards, designing what the poor want, not what the designer thinks.

Many big companies believe that if they just made products in smaller packs or with less features, they would be cheaper and therefore would sell well to the BOP. But it is a lot more complicated than that. Henry Ford created the automobile, but he also created the first $5 workday in an attempt to help create a middle class that could afford to buy his cars. That is what is needed at the BOP. To create consumption, you need to increase people' incomes through jobs. To create jobs, you need to invest in training local entrepreneurs. Also, as indicated, a good market needs logistics, roads, and good government. If we include the poor in our supply chain as workers, distributors, sales agents, and service providers, we can begin to create vibrant and sustainable BOP economies.

Solutions I

Fortunately, some successful collaborative companies seem to be emerging from within the BOP itself.

World Toilet Organization's (WTO) SaniShop: This micro-franchising program trains local entrepreneurs to sell affordable, simple on-site sanitation systems and toilets at an affordable price of $45 per family. Starting from Cambodia, SaniShop is now in India, Vietnam, and South Africa, and going into Mozambique, Nigeria, Philippines, Myanmar, and Indonesia.

Unilever has partnered with the WTO in the form of Domestos Toilet Academy to create a wonderful win–win situation: More trained SaniShop entrepreneurs will sell more toilets and every new toilet becomes a new market for detergents. The SaniShop creates manufacturing jobs as well as income for commission–sales agents, who are often housewives earning $2 per toilet. Such income also empowers the women's status in the eyes of her husband and mother–in–law. Thus, with good sanitation and hygiene, families save on medical bills, women have income and girls have privacy, and health increases productivity and happiness. Such an entrepreneurial model is also perfectly scalable and replicable.

Amul is one of India's most iconic brands. It's a dairy cooperative based in Gujarat state of India with $2 billion in revenue. The brand is managed by the Gujarat Cooperative Milk Marketing Federation (GCMMF), which is owned by more than 3 million small farmers. More than 80 percent of the profits go directly back to farmers. As a result, Amul, via GCMMF, has radically increased incomes for millions of people, and improved the supply of important nutrition and calories for over a billion.

Living Goods: A rural distribution of consumer goods uses an Avon-like network of independent entrepreneurs in rural areas, who make modest incomes going to door-to-door selling affordable bed nets and clean cook stoves, with quick-sale items like soap and fortified foods. Their microfranchise screened agents are given expert training, strict quality monitoring, branding, a good mix of products, effective promotions, and goods that can be sold at a low price. Franchisees also receive a below-market inventory loan and a free "Business-in-a-Bag" that includes uniforms, signs, a locker, and basic health and business tools. Living Goods' success lies in its wide spectrum of products, and creating an "economy of scale" in driving up total sales.

M-Pesa is currently the most developed mobile phone payment system in the world, allowing users easy deposit, withdrawal, and transfer of money with a mobile device.

SELCO has installed solar systems in more than 125,000 homes in India, even though two-thirds of its customers live on less than $3–4 per day. Everyone is charged the same rate for the solar panel, about $450 for a 40-watt system that can light many 7-watt bulbs for four hours between charges. Fewer than 10 percent of the company's customers default in their installment payment and about $20 million has been made available by lenders to finance this venture.

SELCO has even created a small army of entrepreneurs who use the solar panels to charge numerous small batteries that they then lend to street vendors at a profit.

Grameen Shakti is even larger, installing 1,000 solar home systems in rural Bangladesh, where 80 percent of the country's population lives. It has installed a total of 1 million solar systems and will install a second million systems by 2016. Serving a rural clientele means doing business with customers with low and unsteady incomes. They often lack bank accounts; telephones; and insurance against illness, floods, and storms. Solar prices are coming down and kerosene prices are going up, so Grameen Shakti provides the poor with an affordable microfinance loan. The debtors can afford the solar systems, and the payments, because they double their monthly income when they can use solar-supplied light to work after dusk.

BRAC, the biggest self-sustainable NGO in the world, serves 35 percent of Bangladesh's population. BRAC operates 18 financially and socially profitable enterprises, across health, agriculture, livestock, fisheries, education, green energy, printing, and retail sectors. By targeting profitable and scalable businesses, BRAC enterprises are able to increase job opportunities and improve people's livelihoods. The cumulative surplus funds from BRAC enterprises combine to help subsidize less profitable social development programs.

Each of these social enterprises above focuses on not only profit but social impact as a priority. They often start with a philanthropic grant that helps them to set up through the initial gestation period and early learning curve. Once matured in a location, these models generally take on a life of their own as locals learn to operate them profitably themselves and become independent entrepreneurs. Such healthy competition ultimately generates jobs, lowers prices, and boosts local innovation.

So maybe the question is: How did these companies succeed when Western-initiated ideas have experienced either limited success or outright failure?

Solutions II: Aspiration Marketing

Traditionally, the humanitarian sector views the poor as rational people who have little choice but to accept and appreciate whatever products and services are offered to them. This fails to recognize that the poor have feelings and aspirations, too. People are people, and marketing to the poor is no different than marketing branded goods to the rich and middle-class. When they watch TV, they do know what they are missing and wish they had nice consumer items too.

Regardless of whether they are rich or poor, people buy emotionally and justify it rationally. Therefore, when selling to the BOP, it similarly works to sell emotions like love, social status, ego, fear, filial piety, sexiness (including aesthetic appeal), safety from gossip/"face saving," social acceptance, jealousy, fear, angst, individualism, community respect, and, of course, a better future for one's children.

That said, when dealing with the BOP, experience also shows that we have an extra layer of work if we are to make the sale: We need to provide the rational justification for the purchase in terms of functionality, convenience, health, hygiene, time saving, space saving, altruism, and so on. For example, the World Toilet Organization has been effective in promoting toilets to villagers as a status symbol while at the same time helping villagers understand the value of using proper toilets instead of open defecation.

In fact, this concept is not a stranger in the first world. We buy the things we don't need to impress the people we don't like. The poor are similar to the rich in that they do not like being looked down upon by their neighbors. Combining emotions and aspirations with rationality in decision making can be a great motivator if we use it for the greater good in the BOP.

The Next Level: Cross-Sector Collaboration

It is encouraging to see the recent proliferation of interesting platforms serving the BOP. Here are some of note:

BoP Hub (Singapore): Observing that most established social entrepreneurs have never actually gone global because of their weak back-office capacity, the BoP Hub was created in Singapore to help scale up the growth of existing proven social businesses models from Ashoka Fellows and other social entrepreneurs. Instead of implementing programs directly, it serves the entire BOP community by filling in the gaps in the market, through the co-creation of a BOP Shared Services Center and Accelerator.

Acting as a business process outsourcing center, BoP Hub takes over from each stakeholder the aspects of support services that they are uncompetitive in, such as R&D, design, product-prototyping, legal advice, financing, fund-raising, testing, due diligence, logistics, and so forth; this allows them to focus on their strong areas, often in business development, local productions, and implementation on the ground.

Like BRAC, BoP Hub's role is in integrating the entire supply chain of the whole BOP marketplace by inviting multinational corporations, social entrepreneurs, philanthropists, technologists, and academia to join in on for specific projects. Stakeholders share their strength and complement each others' weaknesses. The synergy in cutting time/money wastages and duplications is enormous as compared to current operation by individual silos.

BOP World Design Center is a new, 65,000-square-foot industrial complex that will coordinate collaborative efforts physically as well as virtually between Singapore and global partners and stakeholders. This facility will support industrial design, 3D printing, and business models development, and it will operate as a Timeless Zone 24 hours a day, 7 days a week so that it straddles and collaborates with all time zones in a continuous manner globally.

The convergence of both economic and social objectives at the Design Center will bring solutions that are replicable, scalable, and self-sustainable. This is the essence of how entrepreneurship is changing the BOP. Essentially, what we are trying to do is duplicate the lessons from how Singapore transformed from third-world to first-world within a span of 25 years—between 1965 and 1990—a living showcase of how the market works better than charity aid.

The Abdul Latif Jameel Poverty Action Lab (J-PAL) at the Massachusetts Institute of Technology is a global network of researchers using randomized evaluations to answer critical policy questions in the fight against poverty. J-PAL's mission is to reduce poverty by ensuring that policy is based on scientific evidence and research is translated into action. The activities include:

- **Conducting rigorous impact evaluations:** Using randomized evaluations to test and improve the effectiveness of programs and policies aimed at reducing poverty
- **Policy outreach:** The policy group analyzes and disseminates research results and builds partnerships with policymakers to ensure that policy is driven by evidence and effective programs are scaled up
- **Capacity building:** Equips practitioners with the expertise to carry out their own rigorous evaluations through training courses and joint research projects

Stanford DLab specializes in the "frugal innovation" process of reducing design and cost of a good or service by removing nonessential features, increasing durability, introducing unconventional distribution channels, and increasing volume to improve total profit. Such services and products need to be acceptable in quality and affordable to the BOP. Several U.S. universities have programs that develop frugal solutions. Such efforts include the **Frugal Innovation Lab at Santa Clara University**.

The BoP Innovation Center facilitates sustainable innovations in BOP markets in the water, food, and energy sectors. Its BOP innovation cycle builds on the BOP Protocol developed by Stuart Hart, Cornell University professor and founder of the BoP Learning Lab Network. Bringing partnerships between multinational corporations and BOP communities, the BoP protocol uses a unique set of business tools and practices to engage in listening and mutual dialogue with BOP communities. It co-creates new business models adapted to local cultural norms, as well as co-designs and launches BoP businesses that create value for all partners.

As you can see from the above, there is a growing trend of new innovative players coming into the BOP sector, and this is very encouraging.

A Peek into the Future

Despite the good news, it is smart to be circumspect about the future so that we can avoid repeating old mistakes. If we ponder for a moment what happens when 3 billion people pollute the Earth and deplete its resources so badly, what would happen if we bring another 4 billion people out of poverty to join them? If predictions are true, population will peak at 8.3 billion by 2030. Can the planet withstand abuse by all 8.3 billion people? Certainly not. That is why, right now, we have to seize this opportunity to redefine the meaning of success in human and environmental context.

With challenges come opportunities, and ours is this: If a more equitable world is our goal, if helping the Base of the Pyramid escape poverty is our mission, then creating a vibrant marketplace within the BOP also gives us the chance to market sustainability, simplicity, and frugality as the new norm. These values would not only resonate with the poor, but would be easier on the planet.

Instead of competing to see who has more money, we need to have people competing to contribute to balance. The old billionaire simply had $1 billion. The new billionaire just may be the person who has improved the lives of 1 billion people. In the future, let's hope that there will not be a Base or Top of the Pyramid. In fact, in a more sustainable world with social justice, let's strive for a world where there will be no pyramid at all.

■ ■ ■

 Widely known as Mr. Toilet, **Jack Sim** broke the global taboo of toilets and sanitation by bringing the agenda to the global media stage with his unique mix of humor and serious facts. After attaining financial independence at the age of 40 as a businessman, he decided to devote the rest of his life to social work. In 1998, he established the Restroom Association of Singapore (RAS). In 2001, he created the World Toilet Organization (WTO) as a global network and service platform for toilet associations to promote sound sanitation and public health policies.

He created the World Toilet Summit series, which has been hosted in Singapore 2001, Seoul 2002, Taipei 2002, Beijing 2004, Belfast 2005, Moscow 2006, New Delhi 2007, Macau 2008, Singapore 2009, Philadelphia 2010, Hainan 2011, Durban 2012, and in Solo, Indonesia 2013. Among other things, Jack has been awarded:

- 2006, the Social Entrepreneur of the Year awarded by the Schwab Foundation of Switzerland and became a Schwab Fellow of the World Economic Forum.
- 2007, first Singaporean elected to be an Ashoka Global Fellow.
- 2008, Asian Development Bank names him an ADB Water Champion.
- 2008, appointed to the World Economic Forum's Global Agenda Council for Water Security and the GAC for Social Entrepreneurship. *Time* magazine named him Hero of the Environment in 2008.

SECTION III

The Toolkit

CHAPTER 8

Hello Entrepreneurs, Goodbye Borders

Baybars Altuntas

Baybars Altuntas is an entrepreneur, a shark on the Turkish version of the TV show Shark Tank *("Dragons' Den"), a best-selling author, the president of the Business Angels Association of Turkey, and a board member of the European Business Angels Network. Baybars Altuntas is also the Ambassador of the World Entrepreneurship Forum to Turkey and Balkan countries. For more information, visit baybarsaltuntas.com.*

> War against a foreign country only happens when the moneyed classes think they are going to profit from it.
>
> —George Orwell

That we are living in an accelerated, interconnected, global, e-conomy is no secret. The world is getting smaller, information is travelling faster, people are getting smarter, and ideas are spreading more quickly. Not very long ago, of course, the world was much different. Split into two competing economic and political systems, East was East and West was West and never the twain shall meet.

The world then was bipolar: Democracy and capitalism were at odds with totalitarianism and communism. Those stuck behind the Iron Curtain were in fact stuck; there was no getting out. People and ideas and money were where they were and moving them to new places was almost impossible. An entrepreneur starting a business (say, a shopkeeper in Albania) was, necessarily, isolated. Stuck in

*whatever geographic area he or she happened to be born in, the entrepreneur of
yesteryear had to create a business that, almost always, had to meet the needs of the
micro-local market. He or she was as frozen as the rest of the world, stifled by a
cold war.*

And then everything changed.

*The Berlin Wall fell. The Soviet Union disintegrated. China made a capitalistic
turn and let a hundred billionaires bloom. The Internet was born and high-speed
Internet came along shortly thereafter. Amazon.com invented e-commerce. Soon there
was Facebook, and not long after, Twitter was fueling the Arab Spring. A new,
interconnected, always-on digital world quickly left the old analogue paradigms in the
rear-view mirror.*

*For the entrepreneur, the change could not be more profound. Our friend in
Albania no longer has no choice but to be a local shopkeeper. Changing values, the
triumph of capitalism, the success of the entrepreneur, global access to communication, and the advent of the Internet have all combined to mean that the shopkeeper
could, for instance, become an e-commerce mogul, selling Albanian rugs on eBay,
or his website, or via Facebook, or wherever.*

*The other significant change this new world has wrought is its effect on the
nation-state—a transformation yet under the radar. But make no mistake about it,
in the process of all of this interconnectedness, old borders are becoming less
important. Oh sure, we still have nations, and will continue to, but increasingly,
the entrepreneurs of today—especially the young entrepreneurs of today—identify
as much with being citizens of the world—with being global entrepreneurs—as
they do with being citizens of their country. And the fact that they are actually
connected to the rest of the world with something as simple as the mobile phone in
their pocket means that the global is trumping the local every day, every moment,
right now, this second.*

*This change in attitude, and the creeping worldwide success of entrepreneurship
in all of its forms, is and will have profound effects on countries around the world. For
as people become ever more tied in economically, as they begin to think that their
entrepreneurial dream is maybe more important than centuries-old grudges, the world
will become even more interconnected. When you are an entrepreneur in South
America who sells her wares online via fiber optics made in America to customers who
live in Europe and Africa, borders do mean less.*

This is what we mean by hello entrepreneurs, goodbye borders.

■ ■ ■

How I Got This Way

My name is Baybars Altuntas and I am an entrepreneur from Turkey. I am a living example of this new, borderless, entrepreneurial economy. I am 43 years old now, but 26 years ago, in 1987, I had just graduated from high school. I was working as a sales assistant selling airline tickets at a travel agency in Istanbul. The first thing I learned at my new job was how to use a Telex machine. We would use it to send passenger information to the airlines. I thought the Telex was sufficient for our needs, but apparently it was not. It was but a few months later that we ditched our Telex for a new fangled device called a "fax machine." I tell you, that fax machine was marvelous! With it, you could send documents in their entirety through the system all at once. I understood how to use the machine well enough, but my boss, a man in his sixties, didn't completely trust it. He would have us send a fax and then phone the airlines so together we would go over the contents of the fax to ensure everything had transmitted.

A few years later, in 1991, I founded the Turkish Franchising Association. While working there I received a request from the Turkish media for a list of companies that wanted to do business in Turkey. I remember this request like it happened yesterday. Given the fact that the possibility of an online search via Google had yet to be invented, I had to physically search and create such a list by scouring publishers and bookstores one at a time. I finally found a book in an antique bookstore called *The Franchising Handbook*. It cost me next to nothing. From it, I compiled a list of 100 global franchising companies for the Turkish media and sent it off.

A couple of weeks after that, we began to receive phone calls from angry readers. It seems that most of the companies listed had gone out of business prior to World War II, and most of the area codes had changed 50 years ago. I had failed to notice that the book's publication date was 1922! (I was only off by 70 years or so.) So basically, I was promoting companies that had been closed for years. Oops.

The point is this: I went from Telex to fax to the Internet in just eight short years. Twenty years ago finding information was a skill, but today it is not. Nearly all of us use a smart phone, so gathering information is as easy as a Google search. The issue today then is not whether you know how to find information, but rather whether you know what to do with all of the information that is so readily available.

People used to blame their lack of success on where they lived, but today, in this new world, there is no excuse. Today, everyone is responsible for his or her own successes and failures. Example: I was invited to speak about entrepreneurship at a conference held at a university in the Northern Turkish Republic of Cyprus. During the open forum a student said to me, "Mr Altuntas, you have been here explaining how to become an entrepreneur, but as far as I can see no one in the world except us Turks know we even exist. There is an embargo against us and we can't even export our own oranges. With these conditions in mind doesn't everything you say lose its value?" I gave him the short answer, "Is there an embargo on using the Internet too?'"

So the answer is no, now there are no excuses for an entrepreneur's lack of success. If you have a good business idea, the Internet is readily available. So what are you waiting for? All you need is a computer, an Internet connection, a smart idea, and away you go.

In 1992, I was tutoring my university classmates for a little pocket money. I used $400 of the money I had earned to place a tiny ad in the newspaper. Off that ad I made an amazing $100,000 in just one month's time. Thirty-six short months later I became the owner of a brand new BMW, and was able to hire myself a driver to boot.

The thing is, not so long ago, stories like mine used to be rare, but now they are not. Just last month, one of my franchisees used their credit card to place a $100 ad on Facebook and made $25,000 in sales from it. I didn't have those options available to me in 1992 because Turkey didn't even have a credit card system at that time. Essentially, what I am trying to say is this: If you have a great business idea, you don't need money to get started. That is why I say, "Sell first, spend later."

If you combine information, visual intelligence (the ability to create something that is designed well and is visually appealing), and the spirit of an entrepreneur, you can make the world your customer. It has never been easier than it is now. In this digital age a new vision has emerged that is opening doors to investments and creating a borderless economy. As a result of this vision, an opportunity has been given to each and every person of the world. If you have a great idea, run with it. Don't sit back and make excuses.

There is a saying in Turkey, "If you have honey, the flies will come." Your honey is your business idea. If it is a good idea, it doesn't matter where in the world you are anymore. All you need is single idea and the gumption to take a chance in order to be successful.

Peace in Our Time?

On April 26, 2010, President Barack Obama held the first Presidential Summit on Entrepreneurship. At the summit, he underlined the importance of entrepreneurs and of the Internet as an economic tool for the twenty-first century. I was fortunate enough to get to be a guest at that event. It was amazing.

Prior to his election, President Obama's team did a survey that showed that 70 percent of Americans blamed big business for the world's economic crisis. On the other hand, the same people also believed that small business and entrepreneurs would be the ones that would most likely solve the economic crisis and grow the economy. It really is not surprising then that President Obama declared the twenty-first century to be the "Century of Entrepreneurship." Polls showed what has been clear for some time: Entrepreneurship is an idea whose time has come.

There are many benefits to this idea and declaration, many of which are discussed throughout this book, but let's look at an important one right now: Countries that are capitalistic tend not to go to war against each other. It has long been known that, generally speaking, democracies do not go to war against one another, but what is now being understood is that entrepreneurship and capitalism are further brakes on the causes of armed conflict.

In his highly influential Columbia University article "The Capitalist Peace," Professor Erik Gartze explains that "warfare results from two stages of interaction. First, states must possess the willingness and ability to compete. Second, states must be unable, or unwilling, to resolve differences through diplomatic means." But entrepreneurship and capitalism counter those forces, according to Gartze, for a few reasons, including:

1. Capitalist countries have compatible interests, and therefore, it usually will hurt their economies more than it would help their countries if they went to war
2. Entrepreneurship creates cross-cultural ties that both foster better communication and also offer different ways to compete, short of armed conflict

The up-shot is that if this really is going to be the "Century of Entrepreneurship," then one significant result is that there may actually really be a "peace dividend." It just may be that entrepreneurship will cause this century to be far more peaceful than the last.

So maybe the statement "Goodbye borders" is really not so far-fetched. The ascendency of entrepreneurial capitalism is making it so the people are more dependent and interdependent, have more in common, communicate more with one another, and need each other (at least financially) more than ever before.

The New Digital Economic Age

If this premise is true, that entrepreneurship can help create a better, more peaceful, more affluent world, then it is incumbent upon us to make it easier for entrepreneurs to start their businesses and live their dreams. A Century of Entrepreneurship begins by creating entrepreneurs, and you do that by getting them the money they need to launch their venture. That's step one, and that is what I personally am committed to.

A powerful combination of good ideas, software, and visual intelli-gence, supported by smart finance, has changed the world already this past decade and fostered this idea of an Entrepreneurial Century. It is the Digital Economic Age, as I like to say. Just witness the birth and growth of companies like Facebook, Twitter, and Amazon. These great digital businesses have several things in common, but let me highlight two. First, they were created by young entrepreneurs who had a good idea and expanded it with the Internet and visual intelligence so that it appealed to customers around the world.

Second, they worked with angel investors.

There is no doubt that the need for angel investors has grown as entrepreneurship has expanded. Nowadays, it isn't easy to get a loan from a bank. Banks traditionally gave loans to entrepreneurs if they had a good idea, a good team, a plan, and a vision, but that doesn't happen as easily today as it did a decade ago. The White House realized this and that is why they invited both entrepreneurs *and* angel investors to the entrepreneurial summit. They were laying out the formula for success in the twenty-first century: **Ideas + software + visual intelligence + angel investors = entrepreneurial success and economic growth.**

Angel Investors: The Where, What, Why, How, and Who

Twenty billion dollars was invested by 250,000 angel investors in the United States in 2012. In Europe, 75,000 angel investors invested 5 billion Euros. This prompts a host of questions: Who are these people? Why are they important, and what kind of support are they able to give to the entrepreneurial revolution? Is there a difference between angel investors and other investors? Why are governments so interested in these people? And why should you care?

Let's answer that last question first. Angel investors are a key element in the entrepreneurial food chain. They offer the funds that allow entrepreneurs the ability to start, thrive, and grow. If we are going to have a century of entrepreneurship, we are going to also need a century of angels. It's easy to see why governments would be interested in the angel investing system. Every start-up hires around five people. That translates into millions of new jobs in Europe and the United States. The angel investor therefore is not only an angel for individual entrepreneurs, not just the enabler of new businesses, not just the creator of new jobs, but in a very real sense, they are also the angels of their own economies.

The most important stage in the cycle from entrepreneur to enterprise is the financing of the business model. A bank doesn't really help you with your business, they lend you money. The bank gets paid back (usually) whether you succeed or fail. Entrepreneurs are charged the same amount regardless of success or failure. And, like entrepreneurs, banks want to make a profit. They do so by lending and charging interest. They don't make more if you win. Banks do business like this because they are accountable to their members for the money they lend. That is why they also typically request a security interest or guarantee from entrepreneurs. They want to make safe, smart, secured loans.

On the other hand, angel investors give their own money to entrepreneurs, and thus they have a more personal, vested interest in the success of the entrepreneur. They don't charge interest but instead become an equity business partner. As a business partner, they bring a lot to the table such as networking, experience, knowledge, and so on. But the most important skill they offer is the ability to create a strategy to help the business appreciate. And while it is typically difficult for entrepreneurs to get involved with global investments, with an angel investor's help, that too is much easier.

> Equity is an ownership interest. If you own a house worth $100,000 and owe the bank $75,000, $25,000 is your equity. Angel investors exchange cash for an equity, or ownership, stake in a business.

So where does one find these angels? The easiest way these days, not surprisingly, is through the Internet. Let's start with the three world organizations that bring together angel investors and entrepreneurs. In the United States, the Angel Capital Association (ACA) acts as an umbrella of 75,000 angel investors for entrepreneurs. Within its head office in Brussels, the European Business Angels Network (EBAN) is the umbrella of 25,000 angel investors in Europe. Every entrepreneur, in the States or in Europe, can find an investor from either of their websites. The third organization is Gust. Gust is located in the United States and brings angel investors and entrepreneurs together. They provide the opportunity for entrepreneurs to present their business ideas to their member angel investors.

A Google search will provide you with a list of angel networks, but here are a few to help you get started:

- **AngelList:** Here, you create a pitch and select the investors. The investors review your pitch and ask for introductions if they like you.

- **EBAN:** The aforementioned European Business Angels Network. Highly respected.
- **GoBigNetwork:** First, you list your business and get it promoted throughout the site. Second, you gain exposure. Third, hopefully, you meet investors interested in your project.
- **Funding Universe:** Recognized as one of the Inc. 5000 fastest-growing companies in the United States, Funding Universe can help with all aspects of the funding process, not just angel investing.
- **Funded.com:** Similarly, Funded.com can help with all sorts of funding options, again not just angel investing.
- **RaiseMeCapital.com:** One more platform that allows you to access not only thousands of angel investors, but other sources of funding, too.
- **Gust.com:** "The Global Platform for Startup Funding."

What You Really Need to Know about Angel Investors

If you are an entrepreneur, listen carefully to what I am about to say: There are two different levels of angel investors. The first is for the entrepreneur who needs start-up money from $1 to $50,000. If the investor's business card says "seed funding," then they belong to this category and will help you start a business from scratch. But if their business card reads "angel investor," they work in the ranges of $50,000 to $500,000 and help businesses expand. If you have the money for seed funding then you can be your own angel investor. But if you want to make your business grow bigger and faster and you need a mentor, then an angel investor is right for you. You can always add a second angel investor if you want your business to grow even faster.

There are also two basic programs to assist the seed funding process that you need to know about: incubators and accelerators. There are seed funding centers for both and all they require is a promising idea and the possibility of high growth. There are a lot of seed funding centers throughout both Europe and the United States and entrepreneurs can use them as a home for their business. They offer a lot more than offices though. Those accepted can get financial investments and pitch their business ideas to visiting angel investors who help support these centers. Some of them are independently founded on university campuses but are open to all entrepreneurs. You can find out more information about these centers from the European Business and Innovation Center Network (EBN) in Brussels (www.ebn.be).

After the seed-funding step, your next goal is to make a demo. As a matter of fact, once funded, that is your top priority. Usually a demo is expected within six months. When it is finished, it is time to present your demo to the angel investors. There are a couple of different platforms for these presentations. Things like boot camps, deal competitions, and investment forums will get you in front of an angel investor. In order to be a part of these programs you have to pass a preselection process. The preselection judges examine around five entrepreneurs per hour. If you get past that part and find yourself face to face with an angel investor you might gain not only money but knowledge too. You can do all of this by yourself, but most entrepreneurs enter this level already seed funded and are coming from incubation and acceleration centers.

There are two important details you need to be aware of when pitching your idea to angel investors: both the quality of your team and the quality of your presentation. Your pitch is called an elevator pitch and needs to be no more than five minutes long. If you are curious about what these presentations are like, watch a TV show called *Shark Tank* in the United States, or *Dragons' Den* in Canada, Finland, the United Kingdom, and Turkey. In Russia it is called *Capital*, and in Japan, *Tigers*.

Top 10 Things to Know about Angel Investors

I am a Dragon on the Turkish *Dragons' Den* and I would like to pass on some advice in the hope that if you find yourself before an angel investor, you don't leave empty-handed:

1. **Angel investors invest first in the entrepreneur.** It is very important for angel investors to get along with their entrepreneurs. They also want to see how fast the entrepreneur can get the ball rolling and what quality of work he can maintain once he does. Bottom line, angel investors care more about finding the right entrepreneur than finding the right project. Usually a top-notch entrepreneur has an easier time getting an angel investor to invest in a mediocre project than a mediocre entrepreneur has getting an angel investor to invest in a top-notch project.

2. **Angel investors care more about entrepreneurs' presentation than their business idea.** Entrepreneurs need to be careful when they are explaining their business model to angel investors. In less than five minutes they need to break down the project, the return on investment, and an effective growth strategy. Entrepreneurs must master the elevator pitching technique to be successful.

3. **Angel investors want to hear about an exit strategy.** Here's a hint: You will get bonus points from the angel investor the moment you mention an exit strategy. Usually, entrepreneurs fail to do this. Angel investors don't like to be involved in an investment for more than seven years because they want to invest in fresh start-ups. This is accomplished in one of four ways:
   1. Sell all shares to a new entrepreneur
   2. Go public with the company
   3. Sell to venture capitalists
   4. Franchising

   The reason the angel investors care about their exit strategy is that research shows entrepreneurs lose motivation in their business at around seven years, regardless of how much money they make. When that happens, the entrepreneur needs to decide whether he is going to take a leadership role or simply become an employee. If he chooses the leadership role and leaves the work to professionals, then he will be much happier. If he can't make that transition—and most entrepreneurs can't—then he will end up being a low motivation worker. That is the situation that the angel investor wants to avoid. So the best thing for the angel investor to do is to avoid this kind of risk by exiting the business and moving on to a new highly motivated entrepreneur.

4. **You need to know a lot about your angel investor.** You need to do your research when looking for an angel investor. What type of investments has he made in the past? How well does he know your industry and how strong are his connections within that industry? How did other entrepreneurs feel about working with him? How much time can he devote to you? Have his past investments been successful?

5. **It is important to angel investors for the entrepreneurs to have due diligence.** In soccer, all it takes is one wrong move to get a penalty. Let's say the angel investor likes you and thinks you are the

right entrepreneur for him. At that point it is time for the angel to test the validity of your presentation. This is called due diligence. There are very few angel investors who will make a final decision or sign a contract prior to the completion of the due diligence phase. It takes most investors three months of due diligence before they make a decision. That is why the presentation needs to be realistic. Otherwise it will be a waste of time for the entrepreneur and the angel investor.

6. **You need to have four different presentations ready for the angel investor.**
   - First, there needs to be a business plan, no more than 50 pages
   - Then it needs to be condensed into a PowerPoint presentation of about 20 slides
   - Next, turn the PowerPoint presentation into a two-page brief
   - Last but not least, create a five-minute elevator pitch

   If you have these four presentations ready then you can send an email your angel investor when you are ready to meet face to face. And if they request more details, you already have your business plan on hand.

7. **Negotiating a term sheet is the most painful part of the process.** Due to their lack of experience, entrepreneurs are often scared to make term sheets. Actually, there is nothing to be scared of. They only need to educate themselves on the subject. There are many learning centers throughout the world that assist in this process, like EBAN in Europe and ACA in the United States.

In 1996, Larry Page and Sergey Brin were PhD students at Stanford who created a research project in which they analyzed the Internet. The result was a new search engine, *Google.stanford.edu*. The URL *Google.com* was not registered until the next year. And the year after that, 1998, Page and Brin met angel investor Andy Bechtolsheim and gave him a demonstration of Google. Bechtolsheim wrote out a check in the amount of $100,000 to "Google, Inc." According to *Contact* magazine, "The investment created a small dilemma. There was no way to deposit the check since there was no legal entity known as 'Google Inc.' It sat in Larry's desk drawer for a couple of weeks while he and Sergey scrambled to set up a corporation."

8. **You need to learn to speak the same language as your angel investor.** You can research the basic words that angel investors use on the Internet (*bootstrapping, term sheets, exit strategy, deal, return on investment, company valuation, start-up, 10X*).

9. **Angel investors love to invest in the fields of IT and mobile technology.** The reason is that those are the only industries without borders and you can control them from your home. In those investments, Skype is all you need to mentor your entrepreneur. But of course, not all angel investors are running towards IT and mobile technology. There are other angel investor interest areas, such as the service sector, the electronic sector, the publishing sector, the food services sector, and the biotechnology sector.

10. **If you want to lose you investors, do the following things:**
    ◦ Make a bad business plan and presentation
    ◦ Only speak about the product and not the business model
    ◦ Tell them that the system is too complicated for them to understand
    ◦ Tell them that you only want their money
    ◦ Tell them that they just need to trust you and leave the rest to you
    ◦ Make yourself unavailable during the due diligence phase
    ◦ Don't answer the questions they ask and tell them they will understand if they listen to you

Research shows that only 25 percent of propositions from entrepreneurs make it to the next step. So that means out of 100 business propositions, 75 percent of them are eliminated in the first round. From that 25 percent, 30 percent pass the detailed investigation. So basically, out of 100 entrepreneurs, eight are invited to have a face-to-face with an angel investor.

Out of those who get an interview, only about 50 percent will get an offer. That means, out of 100 entrepreneurs, only four will get an offer. Out of those who receive an offer, only half will make it all the way to signing a contract. So now, out of 100 people, only two will receive an investment from an angel investor. What I am trying to tell you is that you need to be persistent. If you don't make it all the way to a contract the first time, learn from your experiences and try again.

Statistics show that out of those who succeed in getting an investment from an angel investor, 1 out of 10 will become extremely successful. That is why angel investors like to work together as a network. It raises their odds. If an angel investor invests $20,000 10 different times in

10 different entrepreneurs, then his odds of success are higher than they would be had he invested $200,000 in one entrepreneur. Investing this way cuts the risk of investment considerably.

Ready, Set, Go!

As one of the new breed of entrepreneurs who is succeeding in this increasingly entrepreneurial, smaller, interconnected world, as a committee member of 1000 Global Companies Meeting with Entrepreneurs Showcase, as an ambassador of the World Entrepreneurship Forum to Turkey and the Balkans, and as a witness to the transformation of entrepreneurship and capital over the past 25 years, what I can say is this: It doesn't matter if you are from the United States, Europe, Asia, or Africa; the world is waiting for your good ideas.

So, to all of the dreamers and doers and entrepreneurs out there, understand that we are all on the same team now, no matter your nationality. That is why we say, "Hello entrepreneurs, goodbye borders!"

■ ■ ■

Baybars Altuntas is the founder of Deulcom International, the first vocational training school of Turkey and named by *The Economist*–Turkey as one of the top 100 franchise companies of Turkey. Deulcom International became one of the fastest growing trademarks of Turkey and was prised by Eurowards. Founder of the Turkish Franchise Association (UFRAD). Introduced the IATA educational system to Turkey. Elected as the Best Businessman–2010.

He was one of the 150 entrepreneurs invited by President Barack Obama to the White House Presedential Summit in Washington, DC. He was the only participant who was given a personal audience with the President before his summit. After the President's speech, CNN International interviewed Baybars Altuntas live at its Washington studios, the only delegate interviewed. He is one of the dragons of Dragons' Den– Turkey, an entrepreneurship TV show. His book *My Way to Dragons' Den* has been a best-seller in Turkey. President of TBAA–Business Angels Association–Turkey. He is a Board and Executive Committee Member at the European Trade Association of Business Angels (ETABA) in Brussels, Belgium, and the Ambassador of the World Entrepreneurship Forum to Turkey and Balkan countries. He is married and has two children.

CHAPTER 9

New Financing for a New Era

David Drake

David Drake is an early-stage equity and debt expert and the founder and chairman of LDJ Capital, a New York City private equity firm, and of The Soho Loft, a global event-driven financial media company.

An investment in knowledge pays the best interest.
—Benjamin Franklin

*T*here is little good that can be said about the Not-So-Great Recession—not only did it throw millions out of work, but it toppled governments and stagnated economies. That said, there were a few proverbial silver linings, especially from an entrepreneurial point of view. For one thing, the vast and long-lasting unemployment rate created a slew of new small business owners, albeit "accidental entrepreneurs," as it were. Indeed, according to the highly regarded Ewing Marion Kauffman Foundation, "Rather than making history for its deep recession and record unemployment, 2009 might instead be remembered as the year business startups reached their highest level in 14 years—even exceeding the number of startups during the peak 1999–2000 technology boom."

Beyond that, with necessity being the mother of invention and all, the recession also resulted in some very creative and interesting innovations, and none more important than in the area of business funding. Prior to the recession, businesses got *funding the way they always had—a dash of the entrepreneur's savings, a scoop of help from friends and family, and a tablespoon of bank loans. But much of that dried up during and after the recession: Banks became far more reluctant to loan, Uncle Joe lost his portfolio in the stock crash, and whatever savings the entrepreneur had was gone in 60 seconds.*

Enter online crowdfunding: The advent of the Internet crowdfunding era is a direct result of the need of entrepreneurs to find new ways to fund the dream. And find one they did, with crowdfunding now becoming a big, big deal.

The Need for New Financing

There is no doubt that the United States and the rest of the world still reel from the economic and psychological after-effects of the global recession of 2008–2012. High levels of personal and public debt, persistent high unemployment, low consumer confidence, declining home values and property foreclosures, rising prices of consumer goods and services, and limited recovery and growth prospects continued to weigh people down. According to a December 2012 *USA Today* survey,[1] Americans still thought they face a cloudy future going into 2013, with 65 percent perceiving economic difficulty. Entrepreneurs too felt the pinch, as traditional financial institutions could not really help with financing, given stricter government regulations and their own tighter internal audit controls.

Financing, from the perspective of an entrepreneur, a small business, or a small or medium-scale enterprise (SME), refers to the act of acquiring or raising funds or capital for operation or expansion purposes. This includes the allocation of money (or assets) over time under conditions of certainty and uncertainty with the aim of getting an expected rate of return.

Financing is essential to the creation and management of a business. It allows for a startup business to go from idea to reality and to buy goods needed for the production of other goods, for the offering of a service,

---

[1] Susan Page, "Poll Finds Americans Weary and Wary Heading into 2013," *USA Today*, January 2, 2013.

or to pursue new projects or ventures apart from what the business currently does.

As indicated, as the recession wore on, traditional financial institutions (read as "banks") had a difficult time providing financing solutions. Interest rates were high, lending was low, and restrictions were many. What were entrepreneurs to do? Many have turned and are turning to alternative, nonbank, solutions—things like factoring, microfinance, business plan competitions, and so on gained favor as traditional lending dried up. Of all of these ideas, the one that has really caught fire is crowdfunding.

> Jonah wanted to create a restaurant. Unable to get a bank loan, he turned to the crowdfunding site Kickstarter. His month-long campaign resulted in his raising over $15,000—enough to get started. Among the benefits he offered people for "donating" to his project, Jonah named sandwiches after anyone who gave $250 or more.

Typically, there are two ways to raise money for a business venture. *Debt financing* is just that: the entrepreneur takes on debt that he or she must repay. *Equity financing* is where the entrepreneur trades shares of the company in exchange for the capital. Crowdfunding is revolutionary because it basically adds two new ways to fund a business: donations and rewards:

Reward-based crowdfunders are the largest category in terms of the overall number of platforms (that is what Jonah, above, used). Reward-based Internet crowdfunding is the practice of raising funds or capital by leveraging small amounts of money from many people (referred to as the "crowd") in exchange, typically, for some "benefit" offered by the business (as opposed to an equity share or loan to be repaid.) The other type, equity-based crowdfunders, are the fastest-growing category. And while the majority of crowdfunding campaigns are donation-based, equity-based campaigns are much larger in size in terms of average funds raised.

The Crowdfunding Model

There are all sorts of benefits to the crowdfunding model:

- It allows for little or no collateral
- There are less stringent capital rules
- There is less regulatory scrutiny
- It offers much lower interest rates and significantly lower transaction costs
- Services are provided via Internet-based crowdfunding platforms (CFPs)

Crowdfunding for projects and companies is nothing new. A classic example would be back in 1884, when the local government of New York was $100,000 short of funds for the construction of the pedestal for the Statue of Liberty.[2] The newspaper *The New York World*, led by the renowned publisher Joseph Pulitzer, successfully raised the money from the American public during a period of six months via a fundraising campaign. Over 160,000 people donated money, including politicians, businessmen, ordinary citizens, and even children. That is the essence of crowdfunding—getting the funds from the crowd.

In the online arena, however, crowdfunding is quite new—in 1997, fans of the U.K. rock group Marillion ran the first recognized Internet crowdfunding campaign, raising $60,000 to support the band's U.S. tour. Since then, other artists have also reached out to their fan bases and successfully invited supporters to finance their recordings and/or tours. Now, the wider business momentum toward crowdfunding is accelerating intensely and is attracting significant attention because the model disrupts the (finance) supply chain and distribution mechanism that Fortune 1000 companies have built and so vehemently and protected for a century. It is, therefore, a small entrepreneur's dream.

Imagine this: 200,000 dedicated Red Cross blood donors each giving $100 towards the development of a breakthrough leukemia medication. That is $20 million of funding for a worthwhile cause. That's $20 million of funding sourced from the crowd.

---

[2] "The Statue of Liberty and America's Crowdfunding Pioneer," BBC News, April 24, 2013.

Crowdfunding home run: In May 2012, The Soho Loft saw Pebble Watches raise $10,266,846 from 68,929 people in less than 30 days.[3] Ten million dollars! Here is how the story went down: Co-founder Eric Migicovsky walked into Ming Restaurant in Palo Alto, California, during the crowdfunding event[4] dressed in only flip-flops and shorts. The venue was so packed with people in business suits that day that if you took one step in any direction, you would hit something or someone. As Eric finished outlining his success story to the crowd, he shocked the assembled crew by announcing that he was ending his crowdfunding campaign a week early. "We have raised enough capital," he said. It was a historic moment because, as indicated by the announcement, Pebble Watches' campaign had *tripled* the previous world record for financing raised from crowdfunding, previously held by Double Fine Adventure at $3.3 million.[5]

The Potential Impact of Crowdfunding

Private Equity funds, angel networks, and broker dealers are quickly embracing the idea of crowdfunding. According to Jouko Ahvenainen, Chairman and co-founder of Grow VC, "At Grow VC Group, we work with many broker dealers to offer our platform as a service for their use. Through Grow VC they can easily transfer many offline activities and investors to an online marketplace as a strategy to get more investors and make their operations more effective."

With reward-based crowdfunding, the "donors" get no equity in the business—just the reward promised by the entrepreneur, be it a sandwich named after them, a watch, a signed album, or whatever. They do not get equity because crowdfunding for equity is not yet legal (at least in the U.S.), but it looks like that is coming, and the potential impact of it is profound. Figure 9.1 shows the private company growth cycle that typically applies to VCs and private equity firms. Currently, relations and old-boy school associates monopolize these startup opportunities for the

---

[3] "Pebble: E-Paper Watch for iPhone and Android," Kickstarter, May 18, 2012.

[4] The Soho Loft, "Palo Alto Crowd Funding Event," EventBrite, May 9, 2012.

[5] "Double Fine Adventure," Kickstarter, March 14, 2012.

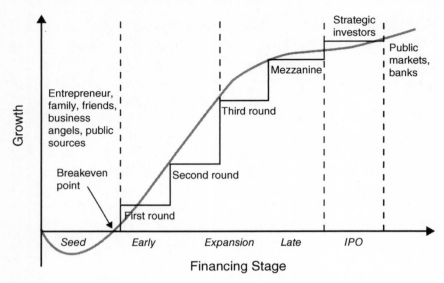

Figure 9.1   Traditional Model of Funding Stages for Companies

benefit of the few. When brought into law, crowdfunding for equity and investing will radically disrupt this model.

The challenge for VCs and private equity companies is to engage in these new modes of capital raising and to identify startups with sound business plans.[6] Bobby Blumenfeld, Executive Director of the Association for Corporate Growth (ACG)'s New York chapter, puts the opportunities in the following terms, "Private equity firms are just looking to invest in strong businesses that can grow. They have the right to choose which companies to finance."

Leading players in the market like Crowdfunder, SeedInvest, CircleUp, Launcht, EarlyShares, Wefunder, Fundable, Indiegogo, RocketHub, and Crowd Valley will be the new broker dealers joining the industry in 2013. These firms are the new blood in the market and are leveraging this technology. "I believe the jury is out on who the winners will be in the long run relative to the crowd platforms," says Steven Cinelli. "Much like an investment bank, issuers will opt for those platforms that build a history of getting deals done. It's all about successful distribution." CircleUp has already done half a dozen projects as a broker dealer with their license held

---

[6]J. J. Colao, "Fred Wilson and the Death of Venture Capital," *Forbes*, May 8, 2012.

by WR Hambrecht + Co. The fact that crowdfunding for equity is delayed pushes these sites to start brokering "Rich Man's Crowd Funding."[7]

The Jumpstart Our Business Startups (JOBS) Act

On April 5, 2012, U.S. President Barack Obama signed into law the Jumpstart Our Business Startups (JOBS) Act.[8] The purpose of the JOBS Act was multifold, but essentially it was designed to allow small investors to fund crowdfunding projects without coming under the purview of the U.S. federal government (the Securities and Exchange Commission, the SEC.) In a nutshell, the goal of the federal JOBS Act was to foster entrepreneurship, put people back to work, put more money in the wallets of working Americans, and do it all without adding a dollar to the deficit.

Some U.S. states have also enacted or are considering their own crowdfunding laws, thereby facilitating intrastate investment offerings that are already exempt from SEC regulation. These state crowdfunding laws include the Invest Kansas Exemption, the Invest Georgia Exemption, and the North Carolina JOBS Act.[9,10]

The amounts that have been raised by crowdfunding are already significant. In 2011, the U.S. crowdfunding market stood at $750 million, and this figure represents half of all capital spent on crowdfunding globally in that year. For 2012, that figure was predicted to close at $1.4 billion.

Crowdfunding Trends All Around the Globe

Needless to say, with crowdfunding being as powerful a platform as it is, it will continue to grow in popularity, and we expect to see it become the funding vehicle of choice for many businesses across the globe. There are an estimated total of 800+ CFPs globally, both in active and in

---

[7] David Drake, "Rich Man's Crowd Funding," *Forbes*, January 15, 2013.

[8] "JOBS or Jumpstart Our Business Startups Act: HR 3606," The Soho Loft, August 7, 2012.

[9] David Drake, "U.S. Leads World In Burgeoning Crowdfunding Trend," *Forbes*, April 12, 2013.

[10] David Drake, "One State Is Leading in Investment Crowdfunding: Guess Which One?" *Forbes*, May 2, 2013.

pre-launch phase. The significant majority of these CFPs are still in North America and Europe, and CFPs continue to develop rapidly in these two continents, but once this growth reaches critical mass we'll soon see any or all of the following scenarios happening:

- A "natural selection" process will occur. Just as the crowd determines which project to support, the crowd will also determine which CFPs will survive and which CFPs will not.
- The "bigger fishes eating the smaller fishes," i.e., successful CFPs taking over or acquiring the unsuccessful ones.
- CFPs forming groups, mergers, or alliances for stability, via resource sharing and even network sharing.

A combination of the following two characteristics can ultimately determine who will get the support of the crowd and survive this rat race:

- **Crowd-friendly user interface:** While crowdfunding, especially equity crowdfunding, is really a complicated process at the back end, it should be easy as pie at the front end. Ideally, if you know how to use the Internet, whether it be as a project creator or as an investor, crowdfunding should be just as easy.
- **Cost-effectiveness:** Higher fees are always a turn-off when you're dealing with the crowd. In order for crowdfunding to reach far and wide, it must be cost-effective. In the first place, this is one reason why it is being preferred over traditional funding sources.

You can imagine how stiff the competition can be if you have 800+ CFPs all concentrated in just two continents of the globe. A CFP has to have a continuous quality supply of both project creators and investors. I don't have to tell you how easy it can be to lose your crowd—it's just a click away.

Crowdfunding unfolding in Asia: In Asia, with its large and socially connected consumer base, crowdfunding is just unfolding. There are, however, quite a few CFPs that have already achieved significant funding goals or are gaining momentum due to their particular flavor of crowdfunding, such as Campfire (in Japan), PitchIn (in Malaysia), SeedAsia (in China), The Spark Project (in the Philippines), and ToGather.Asia (in Singapore).

World giving: A 2012 study on world giving shows the United States and the United Kingdom among the top 10, based on world giving index (WGI) and donating money index (DMI) scores. But while the United States ranked #5 (WGI of 57 percent), better than the United Kingdom's #8 ranking (WGI of 51 percent) in terms of overall giving, in terms of donating money, the United Kingdom ranked #4 overall (DMI of 72 percent), higher than the United States, which ranked #13 (DMI of 57 percent). These findings support the trend in crowdfunding involving the two countries; simply put, the United Kingdom is more willing when it comes to donating money, and crowdfunding is about people donating money to support projects/causes they believe in.

A recent trend among CFPs was the use of big names, such as FundAnything's move to bring in Donald Trump as an investor to attract both investors and project creators. It is too early to tell whether this is an effective strategy, but there is no doubt that you will at least get substantial media coverage if you get reputable people to endorse your platform or if you get a popular Hollywood star like James Franco to start a project on your platform. On the investor side, one would typically rely on investors with a track record of due diligence. On the project creator side, well, if you're a big star, there may be no due diligence necessary for people to support your project—a fan is a fan, and they can blindly support you just because you are James Franco.

"James Franco Seeks $500,000 in Crowdfunding for 'Palo Alto Stories' Trilogy. James Franco is the latest Hollywood big shot to set his sights on crowdfunding, seeking $500,000 from backers on Indiegogo. The star is hoping to adapt his own book of short stories, titled Palo Alto, into a trilogy of films."

(June 17, 2013, *The Hollywood Reporter*)

Understanding the Tool

As indicated, we have seen dozens of successful crowdfunding projects break the million-dollar barrier: Pebble's E-Paper Watch broke $10.9 million last spring, Amanda Palmer's campaign broke $1 million for a music project,[11] Double Fine Adventure raised $3.3 million, and Ouya raised $8.5 million for their gaming consoles, respectively.[12] Venture capitalists (VCs) are nervous. The democracy of the crowd is nibbling at the VC community's heels.

Here are a few fundamentals you need to know about crowdfunding to make it successful for you, along with additional explanations of why crowdfunders make VCs uncomfortable:

1. **Remember that the key word for success in crowdfunding is "crowd":** You have to be able to attract a crowd, and it is best if you have a crowd that is already interested in what you are selling. We work with many crowdfunders but reject working with startups who don't already have a crowd that already listens to them. The reason is simple: customer acquisition cost. Simply, if you have the best gadget in the world but do not already have a fan base—a crowd—it will be difficult to get people to pay attention to you. Imagine you sell meat and decide to mass email 1 million vegetarians. You won't sell anything. What if you don't email anyone? Again you will sell nothing. Get a crowd, or don't launch a crowdfunding campaign if you cannot reach a crowd that will listen to you.

2. **Crowdfunding is a tool:** Crowdfunding is a tool that, in some cases, very efficiently collects and scales the capital for a project at a low cost. If you do look at crowdfunding as a tool, remember that you should not stop using other tools like a fundraising pitch or attending conferences and selling one on one; you will find that crowdfunding is a great accessory to these techniques.

3. **Crowdfunding requires a commitment called marketing:** One crowdfunder we know says he spent four months preparing his marketing campaign for his one-month crowdfunding effort. Indeed, those social media and marketing preparations for months prior to launch are pivotal. You may even need a few full- or part-time staffers

---

[11] "Amanda Palmer: The New Record, Art Book, and Tour," Kickstarter, June 1, 2012.

[12] "OUYA: A New Kind of Video Game Console," Kickstarter, August 9, 2012.

just to manage your social media ecosystem. You need to build demand and awareness of your product, and thus, marketing becomes crucial.

> You can use top social media firms like TeamLauncher and Micro Media Marketing to handle your social media marketing if social media marketing is outside of your core competencies.

4. **Crowdfunding is a financial instrument:** Crowdfunding allows many benefits, aside from the fundraising. It helps us to pre-sell a project, product, or service. It allows us to data mine and manage consumer relations. You can empower your loyal customers and acquire new customers by allowing them to choose the design or color of a product. You can also learn their interests and better understand target demographics. You can even replace part of your focus group budgets with crowdfunding. Yet, most of all, it is wise to view crowdfunding primarily as a financial tool and not as an Internet technology play.

Crowdfunding is not for all, but crowdfunding is making VCs nervous, as they recognize a powerful new financial tool when they see one. Take, for example, these facts that the world's largest rewards-based crowdfunder, Kickstarter, published in 2012. They indicate just what an interesting and uniquely powerful tool crowdfunding has become:

- In 2012, there were 2,241,475 people who pledged money (up 134 percent from 2011) for a total of $319,786,629 (up 221 percent from 2011) and successfully funded 18,109 projects
- People from 177 countries backed projects in 2012. That's 90 percent of the countries of the world
- Of Kickstarter's 13 creative categories: Music had the most funded projects, numbering 5,067; games had the most money pledged, at $83 million; and art, film, music, publishing, and theater each had more than 1,000 funded projects
- Seventeen projects raised $1 million or more in 2012
- Site page views totaled 709 million (up 279 percent from 2011) and unique visitors totaled 86 million (up 252 percent from 2011)

Kickstarter Successes				
Category	Launched	Successful	Pledged	Pledges
Art	3,783	1,837	$10,477,939	155,782
Comics	1,170	542	$ 9,242,233	177,070
Dance	512	381	$ 1,773,304	23,807
Design	1,882	759	$50,124,041	536,469
Fashion	1,659	434	$ 6,317,799	83,067
Film and Video	9,600	3,891	$57,951,878	647,361
Food	1,828	688	$11,117,486	138,204
Games	2,796	911	$83,144,565	1,378,143
Music	9,086	5,067	$34,953,600	522,441
Photography	1,197	427	$ 3,283,635	46,550
Publishing	5,634	1,666	$15,311,251	262,738
Technology	831	312	$29,003,932	270,912
Theater	1,787	1,194	$ 7,084,968	95,225

The Shape of Things to Come

As more and more crowdfunding platforms go online, especially equity-based crowdfunders, we will be seeing more and more startups and SMEs being funded by the general public—the "crowd." Typically and initially, by family and friends and professional connections, and then later, by the others who simply support campaigns and projects that they believe in.

Also, as the number of crowdfunding platforms grow and the technologies and features become standard, the competition will drive transaction costs further down.

Furthermore, as the crowdfunding fever picks up, soon it will not just be smaller business who will be taking advantage of this non-traditional way of funding. Bigger and more established companies will discover that they, too, can leverage crowdfunding to support their business endeavors.

But the best news of all is that entrepreneurs and their startups now have a powerful new tool in their arsenal.

■ ■ ■

 **David Drake's** company, The Soho Loft, through over 250 capital creation events across the globe annually, is enabling firms worldwide to access alternate forms of finance to facilitate corporate growth. As the leading media company in this space, the growth of The Soho Loft has been driven by the universal need for capital that all SMEs seek and for the solutions that The Soho Loft distributes and discusses at its conferences.

Mr. Drake is also the founder and chairman of LDJ Capital in New York City and has been involved in technology media and telecom (TMT), realty, mineral and energy, clean tech, and impact investments for over 20 years. He is a founding board member of CrowdFund Intermediary Regulatory Advocates (CFIRA) and the Association (CFPA). He has an MBA in Finance and an MA in International Law and Economics from George Washington University, where he was awarded the Wallenberg Scholarship for academic merit.

CHAPTER 10

Social Media: The Game Changer

Fadi Sabbagha

Fadi Sabbagha is a Lebanese entrepreneur who founded the new media company Born Interactive in 1996. Born Interactive specializes in social media marketing, web design, Internet strategies, e-commerce, and marketing campaigns.

> Brands are becoming our friends. On social networks like Facebook, on the messaging site Twitter, and through corporate blogs, brands, too, must learn to establish an identity through storytelling.
>
> —Pete Cashmore, CEO, Mashable

*T*he interconnectedness of the crowd is shaping our new e-world in vast, unusual, creative, and some very unexpected ways. From Tahrir Square to Main Street to Wall Street, the newfound ability of people to connect instantly with one another via mobile phones and social networks has become the above-the-fold story of this new century.

This is no less true in the world of entrepreneurship. As we have just seen, crowdfunding has taken start-up funding—indeed all business funding—to a whole new level, allowing people to make their case, connect, and get virtual strangers to invest in the dream. But that is just the tip of the iceberg.

The iceberg itself is social media.

There was a time, not so long ago, when it seemed that social media might have been just another passing fad. The first significant social media site, Myspace, was *mostly a place for kids to hang out. No self-respecting business would really plant much of a flag there. But then Myspace begat Facebook, and Facebook begat LinkedIn, and LinkedIn begat Twitter. Soon thereafter, social media sites of all kinds cropped up all over: Google+, Tumblr, Instagram, Pinterest, Vine, industry-specific social media sites, sites that tried to out-Facebook Facebook . . . and the beat goes on.*

So, to repurpose the words of John F. Kennedy, ask not what social media can do for you; ask what you can do for social media. Because the fact is—whether you like it or not—social media is no passing fancy. It is not a fad. Not only is it here to stay, but it is one of the driving forces that will shape businesses and entrepreneurship for the foreseeable future. It is your ability to build your brand, meet new people, make sales, engage in the conversation, and affect the outcome, all at once. So you better figure out what your social media strategy is going to be because in the entrepreneurial revolution, it is now the bugle that wakes the troops up every day.

Welcome to a Brand New World

If marketing, at its most basic, is your effort to meet and impress potential new customers, as well as connect with existing customers, then social media marketing is especially useful because it allows you to meet new people and get closer to your base in ways that simply cannot be duplicated offline. Right now, on the various social media sites that are out there, your current and potential customers, your fans and foes, your employees and investors, are all conversing. They may be talking about you, or (worse!) they may not be, but of the fact that there is a cacophonous conversation happening online right now there is no doubt. The question, then, is, do you want to be part of it or not? Do you want to shape it or be shaped by it? Do you see that it would be smart to join this robust conversation?

So yes, the marketing game has been changed radically by the advent of social media, and as a result, so have the rules and opportunities. It would, therefore, behoove us to understand the new rules, see how the game is being played, and learn how to win at it.

On Your Mark, Get Set, Go!

Some years ago, social media involvement for businesses may have been considered a distraction. Not today. In this day and age, a solid social media presence has proven to offer a lasting competitive advantage. And, as social media's influence grows, entrepreneurs and companies will recognize it not as a project or department, but as a way of doing business. Soon there will be no way to separate social media from the rest of the enterprise. Thus, getting ahead on managing your social media footprint now can give you a marked head start. The expanding role of social media in business is something I've witnessed daily as an interactive web agency CEO. In this chapter, I share my insights, gained over two decades of experience in online marketing and visibility.

The Door to Influence Is Open

Needless to say, people everywhere are using social media and it seems as if almost every week there's a new social site being launched. In these online social spaces where people meet and chat, there are massive opportunities to ignite engagement and build communities. Social media spaces are a living stage for the global entrepreneurial revolution. They are at the intersection of ideas, business, brands, products, people, and the media; they connect, create, and influence.

Regarding social media, serial entrepreneur and Virgin mogul Sir Richard Branson has written, "In the past few years social media has revolutionized the way businesses interact with customers, making it easier to market new products and maintain a brand's image. By now it's clear that platforms like Facebook, Twitter, and Google+ should be an essential part of customer service. If we need to talk to our customers, we no longer need to limit ourselves to placing ads with established media companies—we can just tell them directly."

Storytelling for Brands: Can You Tell a Story?

Who are you? What's your mission? Behind every entrepreneur and every business, there is a story waiting to be told. Establishing your social media presence begins with telling that story. Today, reaching your market is not about the traditional sales pitch or well-timed campaign, it is, rather, about telling a whole story and generating engagement. In almost all their communications, people tend to resort to analysis to persuade others, even though evidence indicates that people are more effectively moved by stories. To get people to act, even the sharpest analytical reasoning pales before the emotionally charged story.

Why is that? While analysis uses reasoning to teach us how to act, a story uses emotion to teach us how we feel about things, which in turn shows us why we act. The story makes the same point as an analytical statement, but—and this is the important thing—it makes it in a memorable way. No matter how many followers we collect, it is not until we connect with them in some emotional way that we begin to build relationships, and that's why stories—especially in the realm of social media—are so vital. Unless your message resonates with your followers, they won't hear it. That's where the story enters the picture, because if shared correctly, it will resonate with your network and an emotional connection can be forged. So as you contemplate how social media can be used in your entrepreneurial venture, it helps to begin to think about the story you want to share.

One Story, Multiple Media

We live in a complex, globally connected world and use multiple communications platforms for everything we do. Since the Internet has become a media hub that links text, audio, and video 24/7, it is important to consider your storytelling across various media. Each media piece—whether it be a blog, mobile app, or YouTube video—acts as a stand-alone story-telling vehicle, yes, but each also needs to be thought of as part of your larger narrative.

- Online, remember that your story must resonate with your fans, followers, and customers, so tell it in a way that shows them that you two have something in common. Share successes, challenges overcome, and testimonials of people you have helped.
- Use the "About" or "Profile" section of your social media page to tell your story. Post content there that furthers your story. For

example, if you run a business that helps with weight loss, you could easily post a statistic or two on the subject. But consider this: What would happen if you combined those statistics with a story about someone who transformed themselves through your weight loss plan? Exactly. Odds are you would elicit a much stronger reaction amongst your intended audience. That is the power of story.

Co-Creation of Causes and Brands: Leveling the Playing Field

Offline, a big business looks big and a small business looks small. But all that changes when it comes to the online world. There, everyone is created equal, and social media especially has leveled the playing field. You can share, react, and engage just as well (if not better) than any big business. Social media enables you to reach your audience at little cost and enables your fan base to share your posts and market your announcements for you. It puts you in direct contact with those who matter.

Social media cuts out the middleman—you can be the entrepreneur, reach the investor, and gain the audience all at once. You can achieve all that by engaging those who recognize your value and collaborating with them to spread the message.

Clients as Collaborators

Today's online consumers are a different breed. Not content to just shop and go, most expect to experience some sort of engagement with a brand through interaction, participation, and even collaboration. They expect to be part of the story, either by sharing their experience with a business or product or otherwise engaging with that brand via social media. Social media, therefore, is where consumers, through online sharing and collaboration, can participate in the development and success of your product, your business, your brand. You can help them help you by engaging with them and when you do, they will build your brand by sharing your story . . . *if* you tell that story in a compelling way.

User-generated content is at the heart of social media. By listening to their posts and comments you can understand what to offer customers, validate your plans, and gain insights into what works (and what does not) for your business. If you do it right then, your social media followers can become your in-house test market.

To Tap into the Audience, Listen

Assuming you already know who your target client is, you should find out what social media sites they use and which online groups or events they frequent. The idea is to reach out a friendly hand to them in their natural habitat. There you can find meaningful, targeted followers—people and publications who will be interested in your idea. Try to communicate and build relationships with not only people who matter, but anyone who seems to appreciate your story. Even a few relationships can make a huge difference for your bottom line, especially if you're a solopreneur.

Every day, hundreds of millions of people use social networking sites like Facebook, Twitter, LinkedIn, Google+, Pinterest, YouTube, and Instagram. And all of these users are doing the same thing—sharing ideas, insights, content, sites, and products with each other. The beauty and power and challenge of social media is that these people could be recommending your business, too. Your job is to insert yourself into this ongoing and engaging online conversation in such a way such that you become the trusted brand they wish to share with others. As traditional advertising loses some of its credibility in the digital age, the power of online word-of-mouth advertising has become more valuable than ever.

Today, word-of-mouth is word-of-click.

Engage Your Network

There is a huge opportunity in social media to grow your idea or business because these social networks are recommendation door openers: Your clients are probably already on these sites and *want* to share their good experiences with you with their friends. The secret then is to tap into and expand upon this zeitgeist.

The thing then about social media is that, to be successful at it, you must realize that it is a *two-way* conversation. Successful social media users not only listen to what is being said about their business but also take the time to respond to it, based on what they learn along the way. They talk to their followers instead of saying nothing or simply relying on automatic posts. Focus not only on your brand, but on value creation. Adapt your message to your audience and try influencing them rather than directing them. Success takes time. Online communities, like regular communities, take time to develop. But you can develop yours if you take the time to share your stories authentically and communicate with the people who are interested in you and your business.

Responses Build Relationships

So here's the deal: When users approach you on social media, they are seeking both interaction and answers. Do not leave them hanging. Timely responses help to build good relationships, and relationships are a two-way street. You will find that it is rewarding not only to get positive feedback when you start rallying people around your ideas or products, but to give it as well.

On social media platforms, feedback is instantaneous. The more interactive and targeted your posts, the more likely they will be reposted and shared with others. And that is social media gold. Remember, word-of-mouth is now word-of-click. Feedback on any of social platform should be addressed thoughtfully and directly. When you help them achieve their goals, you achieve yours. Inspire, connect, and achieve.

Speed Improves Conversions

Being current on social media is also essential. Post timely content. Users not only like it, they in fact expect it. Live-tweeting during events and posting content about something that just happened spark the conversation.

Social media engagement also relies on consistent interactions to survive. When people comment on your posts, respond quickly. Proving that you are paying attention to your community requires commitment, but the payoff is worth it. Because social media is an ongoing conversation, by promptly responding to and quickly reposting positive feedback, you increase your visibility.

Be sure, too, to promptly respond to negative comments and reviews as well, for these can be deadly to your business or enterprise. Studies show that people will often remove the negative comment if the company in question earnestly works to resolve whatever dispute caused the negative reaction.

Approaches to Social Media

How do you make the most of social media? Here is what works:

Keep it simple: Sometimes keeping it simple is the real recipe for success. Why are you here? What are you trying to say? How is it different from your competitors' posts? Those who are most successful on social media post simple, direct content. Keep your posts short and to the point. Use words that people know and make your approach personal and informal. A compelling photo uploaded from your iPhone with a punchy caption is much more interesting than a long essay about your qualifications. The beauty of photos is that they demand closer inspection. When you post something simple, direct, and interesting, you engage your network.

Stay consistent: Everyone's approach to social media is different. You can employ a variety of strategies depending on the types of products or services you are selling or promoting. For best results, experiment with both content type and posting frequency. In time, you will figure out which strategies give you the best results.

Once you establish a strategy, stick with it. People will recognize you for it and expect you to be consistent. Consistency also keeps you on track and helps you build a loyal following. It can reinforce your unique value through repetition.

Have a plan: Just as large companies have large ad budgets that give them an advantage over small businesses, they also have more resources to invest in their social media programs. This is anything but true for most entrepreneurs, who typically have limited time, money, and resources. The key then is to manage your limited resources wisely, with a plan. Not having a plan is like sailing without a compass. Decide what you want to achieve from your social media efforts and then write out a detailed step-by-step plan.

Perhaps you are hoping to gain more visibility for your company. Maybe your goal is to change your brand's reputation. No matter what the end goal is, having a clear objective for what you want to achieve is important.

Originality counts: Try to be more creative than your competition. Once you find a pattern that works, venture to occasionally break it. Take reasonable risks that do not jeopardize your values or mission, do not require too much time, and can be tested in small doses. The smart money says that thinking outside the box will usually get you noticed.

Originality also involves some risk, and social media has a love-hate relationship with risk. You are expected to take risks by trying new content concepts and playing around with your posting schedule. Yet being at the mercy of your customers can also be risky. It can also be beneficial for your marketing, brand awareness, and customer service efforts.

Understanding Distinct Media

Here is a basic rule all entrepreneurs should remember generally, and specifically when it comes to social media: Follow your customers. If they are on Facebook, then you better be there too. If they tweet, you tweet. One mistake entrepreneurs often make in choosing social media platforms is basing their decision on what they are personally comfortable with, rather than what works for their business. Consider your company's brand, your audience profile, and the relative strengths and weaknesses of each platform before deciding where to focus your efforts. Better yet, find out where your customers hang out online. Post a poll on your website. Have a survey in your business.

A second common mistake is getting overwhelmed by leaping onto multiple platforms at once, or without taking time to understand them. If you are new to social media, it is usually smart to pick one platform and master that one first. And remember, each social media ecosystem has its own culture, rules, language, and rhythm, each of which must be mastered to sustain success. If you do not have a good grasp ahead of time of each social media platform, think twice before jumping onto it.

As indicated, the different social media platforms serve different functions and different audiences. Surveys show that Twitter can be a great site for professionals who want to burnish their reputation and credentials. Facebook, on the other hand, is smart for retail establishments who can use it to post coupons, specials and sales, contests, and the like.

Examining the Competition

Another great thing about social media is its transparency: You can easily see what the competition is doing and, if they are successful, copy it. By identifying what they are doing right, you gain competitive intelligence:

- How engaged are your competitors in social media?
- How many fans do they have?
- How quickly do they respond to posts from consumers?
- Do your competitors have more mentions than you?
- Do their sites get more traffic?
- Do they look and act personable and friendly?

The idea is to gather data on the competition. Analyze it, and adjust accordingly. Knowing your competitors' weaknesses helps. It enables you to fill the gaps in their social media with your presence. Take the social check-in site Foursquare, for example. There, you can find out if your competitors have created unique discounts for users. You can use Facebook, Twitter, LinkedIn, and YouTube for this purpose as well. If your competitors are posting at a slow pace or responding slowly, you can jump on that opportunity to engage potential new customers.

When you gain a strong understanding of your competitors' social presence and what works well in your market, you can locate topics and strategies where your own brand can excel. Seeing what social media presence your competitors are building can help you become an industry leader in your social arena.

Measuring your Return on Investment

One of the challenges with social media is analyzing your return on investment (ROI), because, frankly, it can be nebulous. That said, it is equally true that social media can secure some big wins for your business. Let us say that someone from LinkedIn connects you with a prominent government contact; that would be a big win, right? Or what if a major media outlet finds your business on Facebook and decides to interview you for an article? A high-ranking industry blog can notice your own blog and give you instant recognition by referencing it. Yes, all these things are possible, provided you are putting your name and your company's name out there consistently and intelligently.

Other ways to analyze your social media ROI:

- Hits to your website
- Increased number of Facebook Likes
- More Twitter followers
- Increased blog readership
- Most of all, more money from more deals with more people

Many venture into social media hoping to see a constant ROI. They hope to wake up to an inbox full of product orders and to generate huge revenue fast. Yet it takes time to build social media momentum, and the benefits are there but not always immediate. Long-term value from your social media presence offers benefits at the intersection of marketing, advertising, and branding. Such benefits include brand recognition, cultivating a community, repeat exposure, and demonstrating industry expertise. They also include exercising influence on untapped markets and attracting website traffic.

Tracking your progress: For every social site launched, there are services created to measure and monitor user activity on that site. From specific measurements to qualitative ones, many indicators are available to allow entrepreneurs to measure the reach, clicks, and engagements within the conversations around their brand. Just how much time and effort should social media measurement consume? The only way to know how much social media participation you need is to have some gauge on your return on investment. Though measuring social media ROI may not be easy, it is not impossible either.

Insights into conversions: By listening to your fans and tracking shares and "Likes" you can get a real sense of how your social media pages are converting followers to customers. Analyze why particular posts are successful and double down on those. You can monitor the frequency and volume of responses your content is eliciting, whether manually or by using measurement tools. The more interactions you have, the easier it becomes to see a pattern for inviting positive feedback and predicting what works. Remember to keep your focus on customers' needs and to demonstrate your unique value. Showing is always better than telling.

Be Authentic and Transparent

Online, transparency is essential because there is no place to hide. What you post will directly reflect on you and your business; it is and will become your brand. So post wisely, grasshopper. But remember: Being transparent does not mean sharing every detail of your business with your audience or revealing private or confidential thoughts and projects. Remain professional.

Customers today are empowered to challenge your ideas and products. Your brand can ill afford to make mistakes, as clients will easily be able to express their discontent on social networks. For sustainable success, maintain transparency and open communication, since your customers are smart.

The second piece of advice people are usually given about social media is to be authentic. Authenticity is about being true to your principles, values, brand, and business. It does not mean reflecting your personal ethics but rather the business's identity. If you run a small business or nonprofit whose values happen to perfectly match yours, then you can be 100 percent authentic.

Being authentic in your social media interactions means to be yourself, but with filters. There are some things about who we are or what we do that just are not appropriate to post. Understanding the fine line between being "real" and "too real" is essential.

How to Humanize Your Social Brand

Humanizing your social media presence is critical to forming and growing your community.

Do:

- **Be Proactive:** Tap into the conversations going on in social media. Proactively make an effort to search for the potential fans that haven't found you first.
- **Be Grateful:** Your loyal followers are your cheerleaders. Let them know how much you appreciate their support.

Don't:

- **Ignore Your Followers:** Each follower should feel their voice is being heard. You can thank a group of comments in one fell swoop, but do not let followers fall to the wayside on your pages.
- **Generalize Response Management:** Followers want to know they're interacting with real people. Always personalize your responses.

It is a new world out there and social media has become a driving force, whether that means using Twitter to foment a rebellion or using Facebook to make a million. Both are possible, both have been done. How do you learn how to do what others did? Social media. Find the influencers and see what they are doing. If they did it, so can you.

■　■　■

Fadi Sabbagha is the founder and CEO of Born Interactive. An entrepreneur and interactive communication specialist with over 17 years of experience in the Internet industry and digital media, Fadi combines business, marketing, and management skills with web design, development, planning, e-commerce, and marketing campaigns. He has extensive expertise in digital communications and web on platforms ranging from Web 1.0 to the latest Web 3.0 mobile apps and social influence marketing. Fadi continuously interacts with different cultures and languages and has managed and consulted on projects for clients and target audiences in Asia, the Arabian Gulf, Africa, Europe, and the United States.

CHAPTER 11

Paradigm Shifts in Education

Anna-Lena Johansson

For 17 years, Anna-Lena Johansson worked at the Swedish Employer's Confederation promoting entrepreneurship in the Swedish education system. She now works for Business Region Göteborg, where she is responsible for promoting entrepreneurship, business development, and growth.

If you want one year of prosperity, grow grain.
If you want ten years of prosperity, grow trees.
If you want one hundred years of prosperity, grow people.

—Chinese proverb

*T*he question arises: Where will all of these entrepreneurs come from? For if we are to continue to create a more entrepreneur-friendly global economy, one requirement will be that we incorporate entrepreneurship into our school system more than we have. Some localities are doing just that, while many others are not. But the fact is, we need them to, because the default education system simply does not work to mold the type of creative, independent thinkers needed to succeed in this day and age.

Anna-Lena Johansson would like to thank Per Brohagen from Enterprising Västra Hisingen, Gothenburg, Sweden, and Martin Lackéus from the MORE department, Chalmers University of Technology, Gothenburg, Sweden, for their input into this chapter and interesting discussions.

Consider this story from the New York Times *(June 19, 2013) about the hiring process at Google in the United States. It turns out that Google won't even look at grade point averages, schools, or test scores anymore when looking to make a hire. In an interview with the* New York Times' *Adam Bryant, Google's Senior Vice President of People Operations Laszlo Bock explains that some of the typical metrics of the hiring and recruiting world—the interview, GPA, and test scores—aren't nearly as important as people think. Google doesn't even ask for GPA or test scores from candidates anymore, unless someone is only a year or two out of school, because they don't correlate at all with success at the company. Even for new grads, the correlation is slight, the company has found.*

"Bock has an excellent explanation about why those metrics don't mean much. Academic environments are artificial environments. People who succeed there are sort of finely trained, they're conditioned to succeed in that environment," he says. While in school, people are trained to give specific answers. "It's much more interesting to solve problems where there isn't an obvious answer," Bock says. "You want people who like figuring out stuff where there is no obvious answer."

Google was once also famous for asking incredibly difficult questions during interviews. Things like:

- *"How much should you charge to wash all the windows in Seattle?"*
- *"How many ping-pong balls fit in a school bus?"*
- *"If the probability of observing a car on a highway in 30 minutes is 0.95, what is the probability of observing a car in 10 minutes (assuming constant default probability)?"*
- *"A man pushed his car to a hotel and lost his fortune. What happened?"*

Google does not do this anymore because "they don't predict anything. They serve primarily to make the interviewer feel smart."

(New York Times, June 19, 2013)

So if school itself, as it stands today in most locales, is neither a good creator nor indicator of work success, how do we create students who will think independently and creatively and act more entrepreneurially? Change the school system; that's how.

And here's how.

■   ■   ■

The European Union's Lisbon Strategy, which was adopted in 2000 in an effort to make the EU more competitive, defined eight key competences that were deemed to be more important than others for Europe's future employees and, in the long term, for the future of Europe as a whole. Seven of these were nothing new for teachers, head masters, and education authorities. But the eighth, "sense of initiative and entrepreneurship," made them sit up and think.

Key competences under the Lisbon Strategy:

1. Communication in the mother tongue
2. Communication in foreign languages
3. Mathematical competence and basic competences in science and technology
4. Digital competence
5. Learning to learn
6. Social and civic competences
7. Sense of initiative and entrepreneurship
8. Cultural awareness and expression

It has been clear to many educators the world over for some time that rote education needed to change, and that specifically, entrepreneurship and innovation had to become part of the new agenda at all levels of the education system. As a result, within the EU, the majority of countries now include some sort of entrepreneurial training in their national strategies for lifelong learning. Northern Europe has made the most progress, with several countries, including Sweden, having launched special strategies to promote entrepreneurship within the national curriculum. Two-thirds of European countries now include entrepreneurship in central steering documents for primary and secondary education. At the upper secondary education level, the teaching of entrepreneurship is far more common, and practically all countries have incorporated entrepreneurship into their curricula in some form or another.

Many European countries define specific learning outcomes for entrepreneurship education, which generally includes different aspects such as entrepreneurial attitudes, knowledge, and skills. For younger students, entrepreneurial initiatives are generally more cross-curricular in nature, whereas for older students, entrepreneurship is very often incorporated within compulsory subjects and in a few countries is taught as a separate subject. Only a third of countries have centralized guidelines and teaching materials for entrepreneurship education.

In Asia, initiatives vary as well, from universal political measures to ground-breaking initiatives. It seems that countries in Asia are more comfortable with politically motivated strategies than those in the West.

All countries have one thing in common, however: Their education system is based on their country's culture and values. There are huge global differences in attitudes to learning and the role of the teacher. Trying to agree on a common approach to entrepreneurial learning is tricky. Each country will have to start from its own basic assumptions and devise its own objectives and strategies. In order to promote consistency and transferability, it would, however, be good if there could be agreement on certain common "criteria."

Sweden

One country that was not taken by surprise by the Lisbon Strategy was Sweden. Indeed, when the Lisbon Strategy was adopted, the phenomenon of "enterprise in education" was nothing new in my country; a lot of entrepreneurial initiatives had taken place before we changed the curriculum. Many enterprise promotion organizations were already running short-term projects at various levels within the education system. People realized, however, that the concept of entrepreneurship could encompass far more than what we called "enterprise" and that it could hold the key to at least two problems that were becoming ever more serious:

1. Reduced student motivation at all levels of the education system
2. Fostering the skills that employers say are needed for tomorrow, which are increasingly out of sync with the skills that students are presently acquiring at school

Between 2005 and 2008, a major initiative was implemented in Sweden, which aimed, amongst other things, to draw up regional strategies for entrepreneurship in schools that could be transferred to other regions. A number of regional pilot projects were also implemented. Large numbers of representatives from schools, business and industry, the public sector, and, not least, the academic world met and eventually reached a consensus that exists to this day and that has been endorsed by the new curriculum from 2011:

- Entrepreneurial learning develops specific skills and characteristics such as creativity, curiosity, and self-confidence. These can be of benefit to all future employees.
- Entrepreneurial learning should be integrated as far as possible into the day-to-day curriculum.
- Entrepreneurial learning should be a common theme from pre-school to university.

An entrepreneurial curriculum was thereafter created, and Chapter 1 of the curriculum begins with the "Principles and purpose of the education system." It states clearly that schools must help students develop a mindset that promotes entrepreneurship. Although the curriculum appears to be very forward-looking and modern, it has not yet had an impact at all levels and in all schools.

Finally, after several years, the Swedish National Agency for Education, Skolverket, is now playing an active role in influencing schools and education authorities and, among other things, is offering grants to organizations that promote entrepreneurship to schools that want to improve in this area.

Gothenburg Region

The region of Västra Götaland, of which Gothenburg Region is part, chose to be one of the pilot regions involved. It was very clear during the course of this journey that this area of the country had come a long way in promoting entrepreneurship in various ways through a whole range of different development projects and a number of enterprise promotion organizations that offered services aimed at students of various ages.

Conspicuous in its absence, on the other hand, was the training of teachers and headmasters in how to organize a school that promotes an entrepreneurial approach.

With a few notable exceptions, this type of training was rare in Sweden until the past five years. But with the help of EU funding, a number of different projects were launched to establish training of this type and to demonstrate possible short- and long-term effects. In order to achieve deep-rooted changes rather than just inspiring one or two enthusiastic individuals, the training was directed at the school management team as a whole. And in order to find schools that actually wanted to make changes, it was a requirement that the whole team supported and took part in the training.

Looking back after five years, what are the results? Frankly, in quite a few schools and municipalities, not much has happened, but there are exceptions. In the Gothenburg Region, the municipality of Lerum is a case in point. In 2008, six teams from the municipality took part in a 12-day training initiative that aimed to create an organization that promoted entrepreneurial learning. Thereafter, the municipality's political leaders decided that all teachers and headmasters should undergo training in entrepreneurial education. This initiative makes Lerum unique in Sweden and an example of how schools can be organized in order to achieve the desired entrepreneurial educational effects.

For me, the main impact of having worked with entrepreneurial learning is the greater understanding of the importance of working with teaching that is based on, and which reinforces, students' inner motivation. We also think a lot more about the way we choose to do things in school as it reflects the society we're living in today. We want to give students skills for the future.

The big challenge is to continue to develop in conjunction with the rest of society. Developments in technology and changes within society must be reflected in what we teach in schools (although clearly there must still be plenty of "timeless" knowledge and skills that have always been important and that will continue to be so in the future).

—Christian Jerhov, Headmaster of Rydsbergsskolan, Lerum, Sweden

As mentioned, the Gothenburg Region has come a long way in this field and is implementing entrepreneurial initiatives from the primary level to university. *Framtidsfrön* is a nonprofit organization with associations in various areas of Sweden, including Gothenburg. They train teachers, develop tools, and organize exhibitions and activities for students. Their tools are suitable for pupils from pre-school age to students in their final year of upper secondary education. Each tool is linked to the objectives of the curriculum. Some examples of these tools include:

- *Miljörally* ("Environmental rally," *ages 6–16)*: A web-based environmental challenge in which students and teachers together use their creative skills to solve tasks and problems with an environmental focus from real companies. The work can be done in one or more subjects. The results can be presented in several different ways through an exhibition or on a webpage.
- *Detektiverna* ("The detectives," *ages 6–19)*: A web-based tool designed to stimulate interest in history and the local environment. By comparing new and old photos, pupils pose their own questions to which they then have to find the answers. Their work can then be published on an international webpage that presents detective work carried out all over Europe. This requires students to have drive, to be curious, and to work together as a team.
- *Företagsorienteringen* ("Business orientation," *ages 13–19)*: A tool that involves groups of students visiting local businesses. Visits are carefully prepared and are subsequently presented to the entire class. Students get to find out about local business and industry and this gives a new significance to what they learn in school. The tool is often used as an alternative to or in addition to work placements.
- *Make a Difference (ages 6–16)*: Pupils and teachers take on a reality-based task from associations or organizations that work with social entrepreneurship in order to create added value for the association/organization's target group. Make a Difference can be integrated into most subjects in the school curriculum. The work can be done by the class as a whole or by groups that work on several tasks. Working with Make a Difference gives students the opportunity to use an out-of-school arena as their learning environment. Students work with real challenges and there is at least one recipient that is interested in the students' solutions.

Almost 50 percent of pupils in the Gothenburg Region are currently involved in Framtidsfrön's entrepreneurial activities.

Ung Företagsamhet (UF)

The concept of Ung Företagsamhet, or Young Enterprise, is based on the ideas of the international organization JAW (Junior Achievement World-wide), which has more than 100 member countries worldwide. In Sweden it is a national operation with local associations. UF is the organization that has been active for the longest in the Gothenburg Region and is the most well established. UF offers three concepts, the first two of which have only been operating for over a year:

UF-företagande (UF Business) (ages 17–19): With UF-företagande, or Young Enterprise Business, students jointly decide to set up, run, and close down a business over the course of an academic year. The Young Enterprise Business students devise their own business idea, conduct market research, and obtain start-up capital by selling risk capital shares. Students are given the opportunity to work together as a team, solve problems, make decisions, and take responsibility for their actions. There are also lots of opportunities to take part in regional, national, and international events. Teachers who want to coach and guide Young Enterprise Business students are given basic training that leads to certifi-cation. As well as their teachers, the Young Enterprise Business students can also use external advisers from companies as a sounding board.

There are Young Enterprise Business initiatives in more than half of upper secondary schools in Sweden. In the Gothenburg Region we've been focusing on increasing interest in the Young Enterprise Business scheme for many years now, and this has resulted in an almost 300 percent increase in the number of Young Enterprise Business students since 2005. Consequently, this academic year, some 20 percent of students are running Young Enterprise companies. In terms of the number of students, the Gothenburg Region is the second biggest region.

At university level, entrepreneurship is promoted through four entrepreneurship courses (master's level):

1. Chalmers School of Entrepreneurship
2. Gothenburg International Bioscience Business School (GIBBS)
3. School of Intellectual Capital Management (ICM)
4. Knowledge-Based Entrepreneurship (KBE)

It's crucial for the competitiveness of the Gothenburg Region that the parties involved work together on the development of lifelong learning. That's why links between schools and businesses have been high on the agenda for many years. In order to guarantee the quality of the links between schools and businesses, quality criteria were defined and incorporated in a Declaration of Intent, which was signed in 2002 by, among others, the Gothenburg Region Association of Local Authorities and representatives from industry and trade union organizations.

The Swedish curriculum stipulates that students must acquire a foundation that enables them to make choices regarding their future education and training. This is generally achieved by allowing students to undertake one or more placements in different workplaces. Study visits and visitors in school can also be part of the process. Work placements are usually for secondary school students, but they also feature some upper secondary school courses.

Another link with business and industry is through Transfer, a national organization (NGO) that arranges for speakers from business and industry to talk to students at upper secondary schools. The speakers are employed in all sorts of different jobs in a whole range of different sectors, and all offer their services free of charge. The aim of getting outside speakers to come into schools is to impart knowledge: to encourage students to learn, be enterprising, take initiative, and forge links with business and industry. Talks can be on subjects as diverse as practical leadership, genetics, purchasing, ethics, drama, peace, and conflicts. In western Sweden, almost 120 schools are taking advantage of the opportunity to hear 700 speakers from a whole range of different backgrounds.

How Do You Start from Scratch?

Here's how one of our districts in City of Gothenberg decided to implement an entrepreneurial academic agenda, and how you might, too:

The district of Västra Hisingen has 50,000 inhabitants and is charac-
terized by relatively large socio-economic differences. Parts of the district
are affluent and ethnically homogeneous and have measurable learning
objectives that are well above the national average. Other parts are
relatively poor and ethnically diverse and are well below the national
average in terms of academic achievement.

One of the objectives of the ongoing "Enterprising Västra Hisingen"
EU-funded project is to promote entrepreneurial learning and attitudes
in primary and secondary schools. Eight out of 20 primary and secondary
schools in the district are currently taking part in the project, which takes
place simultaneously on several different levels. It consists of everything
from comprehensive training for all staff to the building of a new school
that will be based on entrepreneurial learning.

In the first year, all teaching staff was given basic information about
entrepreneurial learning and an insight into how to work strategically by
combining entrepreneurial skills with students' learning objectives. In
addition to this more long-term work, the individual schools are involved
in short-term projects of varying sizes that aim to get students to be more
creative, to encourage them to take responsibility for their actions, and to
work together as a team.

One very successful implementation of a type of entrepreneurial
learning that directly challenges the skills of both teachers and students is
Young Storytellers. The concept involves students creating their own
book from initial idea to printed product. Teachers are given full training
to enable them to guide the students through the process. Students take
responsibility for and carry out all of the stages that an author and a
publisher have to go through to publish a book, e.g. proofreading,
adhering to deadlines, and giving feedback on other people's stories, as
well as marketing and sales. The books can be about almost anything.
The most important thing is that it is something the young authors have
a passion for and want to tell other people about. In Västra Hisingen,
1,250 pupils between the ages of 6 and 16, of varying ethnicities,
created just over 1,100 books. (A number of books were even written
in Turkish.)

The finale of Young Storytellers was a book fair held in May 2013,
which was the largest of its kind in the world. Before the fair, the pupils
had discussed how best to market themselves, their books, and their class,
and they themselves were responsible for setting up their stands and

selling their books. One of the main effects of the book fair in particular, it seems, was the sense of community experienced by those who took part in the project. All of the students took part on an equal footing and attended the fair as authors, not students from the "rich or poor" parts of the district. Students from totally different backgrounds networked spontaneously and there was a real sense of pride and accomplishment in their work that day.

Schools in the district are carrying on the work of the book project in an effort to ensure that the process is sustainable in the long term. The Young Storytellers project will be evaluated comprehensively in order to establish how the lessons learned from it can be transferred to a longer-term perspective. The district will take part in a number of EU projects starting in the autumn. The main aim of these projects is to establish how entrepreneurial learning can be measured, which is one of the key challenges for the future.

> Having followed the development of entrepreneurial learning in Sweden for 10 years, I believe that the greatest challenge is to ensure that school management and teachers have a shared vision of what they want to achieve and how they want to achieve it. Also, if we want to be able to influence our politicians in the right direction, we have to be able to demonstrate the impact of entrepreneurial learning in the short and long term.
>
> —Per Brohagen, project manager, Enterprising Västra Hisingen, Gothenburg, Sweden

Thoughts and Reflections

In my experience, using the word "entrepreneurship" in schools is a bit of a sensitive issue. I think it's because this notion is often associated with business and money. For me, entrepreneurship is a way of thinking. It's about developing and exploiting each student's ability, desire, motivation, and willingness to think in a new and different way, to manage risks and opportunities, to be creative and innovative, to get involved, and to take risks and responsibility.

In my discussions with Martin Lackéus, Chalmers University of Technology, Gothenburg, Sweden, he says that "Research talks about positive effects in the form of economic growth, increased well-being, increased competitiveness, more creative individuals with greater self-confidence, greater ability to manage uncertainty and risk, a better understanding of the relevance of education, increased motivation and enjoyment of school and work, greater democracy, greater capacity for organizational revitalization, greater capacity for innovation, impact on equality, and more."

The aim isn't for all students to be entrepreneurs but for more of them to be encouraged to think in an enterprising way, whatever they become when they grow up.

In other words: It requires both a personal and a social investment. Who doesn't want to see more companies being started and growing and to be greeted by, and work with, entrepreneurial bus drivers, engineers, metalworkers, cashiers, and economists?

Clearly, there are a lot of different opinions surrounding entrepreneurial learning. Whatever these may be, today's decision–makers must take responsibility for giving today's students and tomorrow's employees the best possible chances of meeting the challenges that the future may hold. What do we think today's young people need in terms of knowledge and skills to be employable and to be good citizens in the future? What do teachers need in terms of resources, knowledge, and support to teach and guide tomorrow's employees? How and in what way should schools be managed and set up in order to exploit students' potential? Is the current prescriptive way of teaching an obstacle?

Many people claim that "things that get measured get done." Traditional teaching is based on being able to measure knowledge through testing, etc. Entrepreneurial learning is a big challenge because much of the knowledge and skill that is acquired is difficult to assess. How significant are the differences between traditional and entrepreneurial learning? Can they be bridged or combined? How daring and willing are we as parents, politicians, headmasters, and teachers to believe in something that perhaps can't be measured and assessed but that may instead be expressed in the form of a change in behavior, attitudes, and actions?

Is the very word "entrepreneurship" an obstacle in itself? Isn't it really educational development we're talking about here? The Swedish curriculum is excellent; the big challenge is implementing it. Do we have the structure, organization, and leadership that is required for a broad-reaching, long-term impact? I think and hope so. There's a risk however, that a lot of the initiatives that are undertaken "simply tick the entrepreneurship box in the curriculum."

Institutional culture, practice, and policies often get in the way of developing an entrepreneurial spirit and environment within educational systems. Entrepreneurship champions play critical roles but there must also be a strong commitment from the school leadership. Traditionally, schools and universities have been focused on ensuring students can secure future employment. Today, both formal and informal school systems must prepare students to work in a dynamic, rapidly changing entrepreneurial and global environment.

This requires a complete paradigm shift for academia, including changing the fundamentals of how schools operate and their role in society. It requires encouraging and supporting our educational institutions to become more entrepreneurial.

—Karin Wilson, "Educating the Next Wave of Entrepreneurs," in *Entrepreneurship Education in Asia*, eds. Hugh Thomas and Donna Kelley (Northampton, MA: Edward Elgar Publishing, 2011)

I am convinced that the entrepreneurial trend in education is here, but being so new, must be nurtured. This will take time and will require a great deal of effort, patience and, not least, more research.

Here are some of the measures I'd like to see become reality:

- Politicians and decision-makers setting targets and devising strategies at national, regional, and local level and following them up
- Greater collaboration between schools, teacher training institutions, research institutions, and society as a whole in order to keep up-to-date with ongoing skills requirements
- Defining and establishing assessment criteria that take into account both traditional and entrepreneurial learning
- Developing teacher and head teacher training courses that keep people up-to-date with the challenges of the future on an ongoing basis
- Continuously developing the skills of teachers and head teachers
- More sharing of experiences and knowledge at an international level

People say that "the good things are always worth waiting for." But I fear that the wait for a paradigm shift will be a long one. While we're waiting, we need more opportunities to meet together on an international level. The World Entrepreneurship Forum should be a good opportunity in this respect, and one that will make a difference. It's time to make that difference.

■ ■ ■

Anna-Lena Johansson is the head of the Business Development Department, Business Region Göteborg (BRG) (Sweden's second-largest city). BRG is a hub for organizations in the start-up field in the region. BRG has created and runs the growth program "Expedition Forward," in which nearly 700 companies participate. Anna-Lena previously worked at the Swedish Employer's Confederation in different positions during 17 years. One of her main tasks was to promote entrepreneurship in the Swedish education system.

CHAPTER 12

Creating an Entrepreneurial Ecosystem

Nicolas Shea

Nicolas Shea is a Chilean entrepreneur, former innovation and entrepreneurship advisor to the Chilean Minister of Economy (2010–2011), and founder of Start-Up Chile.

> Instead of changing the world through revolution, we can change the world through innovation.
>
> —Juan Andrés Fontaine,
> former Minister of Economy, Chile

*B*illions *of dollars are spent every year by governments to foster entrepreneurship, and boost innovation. The conventional wisdom encourages governments to spend most of the money—if not all—on basic research, infrastructure, and office space. However, in an innovation economy, the game has changed. It is not about the hardware, but the software, and decisions should be made based not on the advantages of the past, but on the prospects for the future. Based not on supply, but on demand. Most importantly, those ideas should not come from "experts" and committees but from the entrepreneurs themselves: folks in the trenches, garages, attics, and basements. Those that Steve Jobs referred to as "rebels" or "crazy ones."*

At a time when the "tyranny of the status quo" in the developed countries is exhausting ideas and sapping energy from the younger generations and when governments are spending billions to block or restrict immigration, it turns out that there are thousands of brilliant, creative, and resilient entrepreneurs who are willing to move elsewhere to get their chance of success—halfway across the world if necessary.

If you invite them, they will come.

Here's how we did it.

An Unexpected Call

It was February 24, 2010. I was working in my home away from home in Stanford, California, when a Skype call popped up on my computer screen. It was none other than Juan Andrés Fontaine, Minister of Economy of Chile for the new government of Sebastián Piñera, and one of the best-known macro-economists in the country. He was calling to invite me to join his staff as "Innovation and Entrepreneurship Advisor." Due to my commitments at the time (company and family) and a strong skepticism of whether I was suited for the job, I could not accept right away, but I agreed to meet him soon thereafter in person. In the meantime, I agreed to put together a preliminary innovation plan for the next four years, regardless of my final decision.

On the eve of February 27, we received word that a magnitude 8.8 earthquake—the fifth largest recorded earthquake in history—had devastated Chile. Being in California at the time, it was impossible to determine the size of the catastrophe and the impact it would have on all our lives. The next morning, we got an email informing us that two tsunamis that came right after the earthquake had swept away miles of coastland, causing hundreds of deaths—among them, two children of a very close cousin. Right then and there the decision was made: My wife and I knew that we had to go home and help in whatever way we could.

The Earthquake

The official figures state that a total of 525 people died and another 370,000 lost their homes in this monstrous disaster. The earth shook mercilessly in a stretch of land that is home to more than 80 percent of the population. In Santiago and other cities, the three-minute earthquake caused power and water outages and damaged vast numbers of homes, including most of the patrimonial buildings and churches which happened to be precisely in the affected area.

The government began distributing food and other basic necessities and sent out troops to maintain order. Because of the decimated infrastructure, many towns and villages were cut off from supplies and, despite the militarization of the zones, widespread looting and hoarding began to happen. Hospitals were forced to close down, and there was even a prison break in Concepción. Estimates of losses to the economy ranged from $15 to $30 billion (10 percent of GDP) and it was quite obvious that rebuilding the country would require a huge effort and a set of new and creative policies to achieve full recovery.

Things seemed desperate. The new government knew that dramatic steps would have to be taken in order to prevent utter chaos.

Inspired by Immersion

> To create an innovation hub, you start with some very bright people, let them hang out with other very bright people, and allow their imaginations to roam.
> —Susan Hockfield, former president of MIT

Inspired by the way Silicon Valley has attracted entrepreneurial talent from across the globe, I reached out to some of my friends in the area. Jim and Marian Adams, as an important part of the Stanford community, were determined to help. When I told them about my new appointment and that I was working on an Innovation Plan, they immediately arranged meetings with some of the most brilliant and supportive people on campus.

In my conversation with Jim, he asked if I had any ideas in mind for my new job. In fact, I did. Over the past year, I had been mulling over the problem of the challenging visa and immigration status of foreign entrepreneurs in the United States, an issue that affected many good friends from Stanford and thousands of others around the country. This is a widespread and common problem for foreign entrepreneurs who would love to start their companies in the United

States, especially in Silicon Valley. The problem is, it is nearly impossible for a foreign graduate to get a visa due to America's stringent immigration and visa policies. As a good American friend says, "How smart is that? We spend billions of dollars subsidizing these unbelievable colleges and institutions that attract and select the best and brightest worldwide, and shortly after graduation, we kick them out of the country!"

So my big idea was this: What if we could motivate some of them to move to Chile, at least for a while? If the plan were successful, we would not only be able to ignite a similar kind of open and collaborative environment to that of Silicon Valley, but we would also be able to jump-start our economy and, in the process, connect ourselves, through these entrepreneurs, to major innovation hubs and markets around the world.

It sounded naive to think that entrepreneurs who had made it to Silicon Valley would agree to move to Chile for a while, but as a bootstrapping entrepreneur myself, I know the feelings around starting a business from scratch and how great the need for financial, intellectual, and emotional support can be. I thought that this crazy plan just might work. So did Jim and Marian.

Jim introduced me to their close friend David Kelley, founder of IDEO and the d.school at Stanford. In a one-hour conversation he told me, "If you want to unleash a wave of innovation, you have to focus on the individual, something simple, concrete, and visual that you can try and scale quickly." That same day I met with Charles Holloway, my former professor of Entrepreneurship at the Stanford Graduate School of Business, who immediately offered his full support. As he liked the immigration idea, he referred me to Steve Ciesinsky and Emil Wang at SRI International. I met with them before flying down to Chile. When I told them about my possible new role in the Chilean government, Steve's advice was, "Before you land in Chile, you must read this book," and he handed me a copy of *Start-Up Nation*, which tells the story of the entrepreneurial revolution in Israel and highlights the fundamental impact of immigrants after the collapse of the Soviet Union. This book was not only an important source of inspiration and validating evidence for the project, but it lead us to create a great brand.

Among other things, *Start-Up Nation* explains the "Israeli miracle." Of the many factors to which this is attributed—attitude (chutzpah), serving in the military, hyper networking, and horizontal hierarchy—the most relevant variable is high skilled immigration. Since 1948, 3 million Jews from over 90 countries have arrived in Israel. In the 1980s and 1990s alone, 850 thousand came from the Soviet Union. As Gidi Grinstein says, "Immigrants are not averse to starting from scratch. They are by definition risk-takers. A nation of immigrants is a nation of entrepreneurs."

So the dots began to connect: We were going to create a reverse brain drain from the United States, and thereafter, a flow[1] of talent between Chile and the rest of the world. In a beautiful, safe, fun, and business-oriented country like ours, we were going to apply the lessons from Silicon Valley and the Israeli entrepreneurial revolution, and we were going to use the power of the government and the sense of urgency and purpose that came with the earthquake to leverage what was needed to launch this bold venture.

Our idea was fairly audacious. If you think about it, granting taxpayer money to foreigners from rich countries who don't even have a vote is the exact opposite of what a traditional politician would do—i.e., spread money wisely among people who do vote. We knew it would be a hard sell. That said, we had a perfect argument to support our idea.

In the mid-nineteenth century, thousands of Europeans migrated to Chile, motivated by the government's offer to grant them land and permanent residence. Today, many of the most successful entrepreneurs and leaders in Chile are descendants of those immigrants and Chileans all know the outcome of that progressive public policy. The positive impact our immigrants have made, both intellectually and culturally, is unquestionable.

The Pitch

The meeting with the new Minister finally took place on March 15. The installation was quite chaotic. All the plans that the new administration had for their starting government had to be postponed suddenly by the

---

[1] Notice "flow," not "stock." Entrepreneurs appreciate the freedom come and go as they wish.

imperious need to put one third of the country back on its feet again after the earthquake. Innovation and entrepreneurship were not the main priority at that moment.

Minister Juan Andrés Fontaine, however, was eager to back fresh ideas that had the potential to accelerate economic growth. He explained to me how innovation was structured within the government and the different actors I should meet before I made up my mind. Back at the Minister's office that afternoon, I told him that I would accept the job and try to integrate all the different actors as if we were one team.

We would call our plan "Innovation Chile," and with it give life to a vision of transforming Chile into the innovation and entrepreneurship hub[2] of Latin America.

As the meeting ended and I was leaving his office, I suggested that we should try to start the program immediately: "Let's invite early-stage entrepreneurs from all over the world, give them support to start their companies from Chile, and see what happens." The Minister immediately understood the direct and indirect impact of such a policy and the value behind connecting Chile to the globe. However, he was skeptical about the quality of entrepreneurs who would be motivated to come to Chile. In economic terms, he feared a strong adverse selection for the wrong entrepreneurs. "We have nothing to lose if we try. Let's set high standards and if no one comes there will be no public spending at all," I argued. He said something like, "Good point, let's see and try." Whatever it was he actually said, what I heard was "green light." The obsession began. As I left his office I had a strong hunch that this would be big.

> The entrepreneur is the single most important variable in the innovation equation.
>
> —Don Valentine, founder of Sequoia Capital

Getting Started

What: Attract (borrow?) the best and the brightest entrepreneurs from the main innovation hubs around the world—starting with Silicon Valley.

---

[2] Notice "hub," not "pole."

Why: Rebuild Chile through entrepreneurship and innovation.

How: Help with all the needs any bootstrapping entrepreneur in a foreign country might have—funds, visas, bank accounts, mentors, access to talent, schools for their children, accommodations, lawyers, accountants, connection to local investors, etc.

How many: 1,000 start-ups by 2014.

How much: $1 million to cover the pilot program of 25 entrepreneurs, $49 million to scale to 1,000.

When: Immediately.

Following Silicon Valley's start-up approach, we designed a prototype centered on the entrepreneur more than on entrepreneurship. In fact, our selection criteria accounts two-thirds for the entrepreneur and her team and one-third for the business model and industry potential. As tempting as it can be to "pick winners" and get involved in strategy and tactics, that is the entrepreneurs' job, not ours. Start-Up Chile is not an incubator, but a community. We don't take ownership; we build long-lasting relationships. Our job is to attract, select, and make sure that, to the best of our abilities, the entrepreneurs that come to Chile have a memorable and valuable experience. Actually, I still question if Start-Up Chile is about entrepreneurship or about attraction of talent. It is both.

During the first year, 9 out of every 10 Chileans were against the idea, and actually considered the plan stupid. Well-known businessmen and innovation experts, not to mention many distinguished government officials, would tell us:

- "This is all we need. Our own government doesn't trust Chilean entrepreneurs."
- "You are lucky if you bring the street sweepers from New York City."
- "High-potential entrepreneurship will never take place in Chile."
- "The entrepreneurs will leave after six months, having spent their best paid vacations, and have zero impact in Chile."
- "For less than $250,000 no one will come."
- And so on.

But we had a vision, a sense of urgency, a purpose, and an extraordinary team. Very early on, my lifelong friend Cristóbal Undurraga resigned from his job at a Silicon Valley start-up to join the Government. As CEO of Innova Chile, a branch of Chile's development agency (Corfo), he was responsible for all governmental innovation initiatives, including Start-Up Chile. In September, Jean Boudeguer, a brilliant IT engineer, joined the team as Start-Up Chile's first executive director. And one by one we built an extraordinary team.[3] As senior government officials we had a lot of power—more than we realized—and we used it wisely.

Global Validation

Back in Silicon Valley, with the approval of the Minister and the funding from Corfo, we needed to show the world that we were serious about transforming Chile into the entrepreneurship and innovation hub of Latin America and convince world-class entrepreneurs that Start-Up Chile was a good choice for their immediate future. We gathered other exceptional leaders from the field of innovation and entrepreneurship, such as Kathy Eisenhardt, Chuck Eesley, Tina Seelig, and Vivek Wadhwa, to whom Chile should always be grateful.

Introduced by our common great friend Raúl Rivera, I met Vivek in Palo Alto after my first trip to Chile. We connected immediately. He had visited Chile in 2009 and shared the same view that high-skilled immigration—not IT outsourcing—was the best path towards development. Vivek has since been a fabulous advocate of Start-Up Chile and has embraced Chile as his own. To give him all the credit he deserves, Start-Up Chile really started getting global attention after his piece in *TechCrunch* in August 2010. That same month, Maureen Farrell wrote about us in *Forbes* and soon we were in the news everywhere.

We were surprised how much press we were receiving and it seemed clear that we had tapped into a global issue. In fact, immigration was not a big deal in Chile, but soon we realized how big and loaded it was in the United States and Europe. In the words of a journalist, "Start-Up Chile is

---

[3] Diego Alcaíno, Matías Rivera, Brenna Loury, Jen Rix, Cristián López, Diego Philippi, Felipe Costabal, Cata Boetsch, Andrea Iruretagoyena, Ignacio Henderson, Roshni Uttamchandani, Horacio Melo, Caro Rossi, Maite Larraechea, Sebastián Vidal, Daniela Lee and many others.

Figure 12.1   The Lure of Chilecon Valley
The Economist, October 2012

the perfect ammunition against stupid policy makers and politicians that are shutting down our borders to foreign talent and don't understand that talent is the key ingredient of the innovation economy."

Our Prototype

> Our time in Chile allowed us to focus on building our prototype and gave us necessary oxygen to operate. It was the best decision we've ever made in the early stage.
>
> —Amit Aharoni,
> first Start-Up Chile entrepreneur

Amit Aharoni and Nicolas Maunier had met in Stanford. Both graduated with honors from Haifa University and l'École Polytechnique de Paris and they were building CruiseWise, an easy-to-use marketplace for the cruise industry. They had come to the United States with the dream of becoming Silicon Valley entrepreneurs, but one month into their final quarter they lacked two basic things: visas and money.

And here's the thing: they were negotiating with three venture capital firms and had a formal offer from one of them for some money and a lot of equity. I told Amit and Nicolas that it would be a mistake for them to sign the term sheet. Instead, I suggested that they come to Chile for six months, all expenses paid by the Chilean government. While in Chile, they would do exactly what they would be doing in the United States—coding, user/market testing, and eating pizza—with the advantage of receiving a lot of attention from people wanting their success. Besides, if things went well, they would have proven a lot and the company's valuation (and the value of their share) should be higher. If things went the other way, they would save time, money, and stress and would be in a good position to move on.

So when they met with their U.S. investor and told him that they were not going to take his money and were instead moving to Chile, the investor said, "Actually it's not such a bad idea. If in six months you come with a good product and you are still committed to the project, you will have eliminated a lot of risk, so I don't see why we would not be interested in investing in your company." The day they arrived to Chile,

Figure 12.2   Amit and Nicolas Arriving in the Santiago Airport

August 2010

Amit and Nicolas appeared with Minister Fontaine in the press and became national celebrities.

After six months, Amit and Nicolas where back in Silicon Valley. They were able to raise money from U.S. and Chilean investors at a valuation of 2.5 times what they were initially offered and they finally got their U.S. working visas. CruiseWise was acquired on May 4, 2013, by TripAdvisor and the team moved to Pennington, New Jersey.

The Measurable Impact (ROI)

By all accounts, Start-Up Chile has been a huge success. After a pilot project of 22 start-ups that arrived between August 2010 and January 2011, Start-Up Chile was officially launched. Since 2011, there have been seven applications processed (plus the pilot program) for 100 spots each. In total, 7,200 applications have been submitted from around 60 different countries and the first application process in 2013 closed on April 9 and had 1,577 applications from 68 countries.

As with European immigration in the nineteenth century, we believe that the most valuable output of Start-Up Chile over time will be the cultural interaction between foreign entrepreneurs with Chileans, which, by the way, is the only explicit thing we require of entrepreneurs. Michael Leatherbee, PhD (c) in innovation at Stanford and secretary general of our advisory board, has already found positive impact among Chilean entrepreneurs. Although hard to measure, it is clear that the cultural impact will be Start-Up Chile's greatest legacy. However, at the end of the day, our funding competes with other governmental initiatives, so if we want the program to last beyond a particular government, we must prove that our return on investment (ROI) is worth the effort.

Chileans' interest in the program has grown, too, as measured by the increasing percentage of Chilean applicants. Although the first two rounds were limited to entrepreneurs residing abroad (including Chileans) the percentage of Chileans applying to the program in the seventh round is up to 40 percent. Although there are many other grants for entrepreneurs in Chile that give up to $100,000, the vast majority prefer to apply to Start-Up Chile because of branding, experience, and global mindset.

Growth

However measured, the growth of Start-Up Chile has been phenomenal.

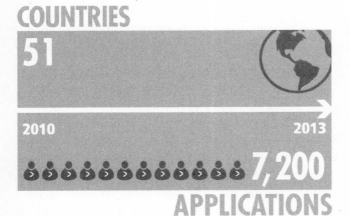

Participants: Out of all of these applicants, we have now hosted 583 start-ups (plus 1,000 entrepreneurs) from 51 different countries. Here are the breakdowns:

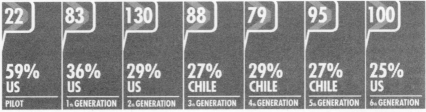

By industry:

1st GENERATION	2nd GENERATION	3rd GENERATION	4th GENERATION	5th GENERATION	6th GENERATION
13% E-Commerce	11% E-Commerce	20% E-Commerce	23% E-Commerce	13% E-Commerce	25% E-Commerce
28% Social Media	32% Social Media	14% Social Media	24% Social Media	24% Social Media	18% Social Media
8% Education	11% Education	18% Education	16% IT & Enterprise Software	14% Education	11% Mobile & Wireless

By stage:

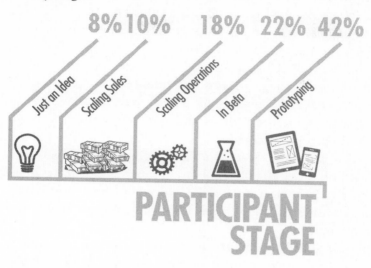

- **Media and PR:** While press coverage has been an important way to attract entrepreneurs, it has also been important to inspire other governments to follow our lead. Start-Up Chile has been featured in *Forbes*, *The Economist*, *TechCrunch*, *The Huffington Post*, *Reuters*, *Bloomberg*, *Exame*, *The Washington Post*, and many other publications. It has inspired Brazil, Peru, Greece, Denmark, Spain, and even the United States to run similar programs. The Chilean press has reacted, and many national outlets launched special supplements and sections devoted to entrepreneurship and tech. We hope those features on successful entrepreneurs shape new role models for the Chilean youth.

In 2010, 20 stories about Start-Up Chile were reported (1 national, 19 international). The numbers rose to a total of 205 stories in 2011 (92 national, 113 international) and grew more than 60 percent in 2012 (172 national, 166 international). In 2013, the press has already run more than 170 stories about the program and its entrepreneurs (100 national, 74 international).

- **Funds raised:** Start-ups supported by Start-Up Chile have risen more than $20 million—40 percent from Chileans.

- **Social impact/Return Value Agenda (RVA):** Start-Up Chile entrepreneurs are required to spend a fundamental part of their life in Chile sharing their skills and knowledge with local entrepreneurs in Chile. Aside from the spontaneous networking and sharing that takes place among Start-Up Chile participants, entrepreneurs commit to several activities with college students, entrepreneurs, and professionals interested in global entrepreneurship. These activities take place in universities, schools, local companies, among others, both in Santiago and the 15 Chilean provinces.

  From what we know, Start-Up Chile entrepreneurs have had a direct impact on over 80,000 Chileans through more than 2,000 activities so far: 595 meet-ups, 1,672 workshops and conferences (486 hosted outside Santiago), and 1,698 hours spent mentoring Chilean entrepreneurs.
- **Direct spending and job creation:** Almost 90 percent of the funds granted by the Chilean government are spent in Chile, both on living expenses and salaries of Chilean employees. Forty percent of entrepreneurs are staying for one year and 25 percent are staying beyond that. On average, Start-Up Chile entrepreneurs hire one Chilean during their stay for $1,500 per month. In addition, entrepreneurs attract around two visitors to our country during their stay, each one around 10 days in Chile with an estimated expenditure of $200 per day. Adding all this up, our estimates indicate that our entrepreneurs spend on average $75,000 in Chile.
- **Global social networking:** In general, Chileans love Chile. It's beautiful, modern, safe, and stable. For a Chilean, this may not be a very noteworthy statement, but for one of the thousand entrepreneurs that we have invited over the past two years, it is. Each one has well above 1,000 connections in their social network, and for around six months, all of their tweets and posts are coming from Chile.

Success Stories

The number of successful startups that have come out of Startup Chile are almost too numerous to mention, but here are some of the highlights:

Safer Taxi (Switzerland): Mobile app to book and pay for cabs in a fast and safe manner. Raised $3.5 million in venture capital funding (Argentina, Brazil, and the United States). They are fully functional in Argentina, Brazil, and Chile.

KienVe (Uruguay): Mobile application that serves as a real-time social network for the second screen. Raised $250,000 in angel investment. Has traction in Paraguay, Uruguay, and Chile, achieving sales of more than $25,000 per month.

RE 3D (United States): With their first product, the Gigabot, they are democratizing 3D printing. Gigabot is already a hit on Kickstarter, where it has raised four times what they intended.

Junar (Argentina): Junar provides a cloud-based platform for opening data to drive innovation, encourage collaboration, and meet legislative goals. They raised $1.2 million in funding from Chile's Aurus and Austral Capital; they are currently working with the state of California.

Taggify (Argentina): Helps monetize your website by displaying contextually relevant ads in the content of your website. Raised $1 million in funding from Chile's Aurus fund and from publisher giant Copesa.

Backyard Brains (United States): Provides a fun, affordable, hands-on way to experiment with neuroscience and allows children to learn how the brain works. They have traveled throughout Chile allowing kids to learn about neuroscience, hopefully inspiring many to become interested in science. They have sold thousands of their "SpikerBox," allowing kids from around the world to discover neuroscience.

Biletu (Chile): Biletu is a mobile app to facilitate payments between friends and avoid the awkwardness by using smart phones. Its Chilean founder, Felipe Millan, is currently in Estonia participating in Startup Wise Guys.

Edoome (Chile): Edoome is an educational social network that seeks to facilitate the management of the classroom and also connect educational institutions. Its Chilean founder, Leonardo de la Fuente, has partnered with the most respectable public schools in Chile, bringing tech solutions for a problem that has turned into a national discussion.

Conclusion

Start-Up Chile is a program designed by the Chilean Ministry of Economy, executed by its Development Agency (Corfo), and funded by Chilean taxpayers, with the purpose of converting Chile into the innovation and entrepreneurship hub of Latin America. Its purpose is to sustain the social and economic development of our country. Although the results are yet to fully be realized, it has been a good use of public funds.

We often get asked the question, "How could Chilean government officials come up with such a well-thought-out public policy?" My best answer is that they didn't. More than a public policy preceded by an iteration of "committees of innovation experts," Start-Up Chile is the story of a group of entrepreneurs who happened to be in government when faced with the titanic challenge of helping their country get back on its feet. It comes from the conviction that "innovation starts with some very bright people, hanging out with other very bright people and allowing their imaginations to roam" and the belief that smart and committed entrepreneurs from all around the globe will recognize, appreciate, support, and move to countries that "get it."

If you are an entrepreneur, business leader, politician, or policy maker, just do it. Start-Up Chile is available to help in any way. If we could, you can. The only thing you must remember is to build your program around the individual. Long-lasting relationships are not built around Memorandums of Understanding or collaboration agreements, but around love and friendship. The best entrepreneurs know that that's what life is about.

■ ■ ■

Nicolas Shea is a Chilean entrepreneur who served as senior advisor for Entrepreneurship and Innovation to the Chilean Minister of Economy in 2010–2011. He is the recipient of two National Innovation Awards for Start-Up Chile (2011) and Cumplo (2012), and Founder of Start-Up Chile, Cumplo, eClass, and the Chilean Association of Entrepreneurs (ASECH). He serves on the board of Start-Up Chile, Socialab, and Fundación Avonni. Holds a B.A. in Business and Economics from Universidad Católica, a MSc in Education from Columbia University, and a MSc in Management from the Stanford Graduate School of Business. He teaches High Potential Entrepreneurship in Universidad Adolfo Ibáñez School of Business and Universidad Católica's School of Design.

Nico lives in Santiago with his wife, Josefa, and their five amazing kids: Josefita, Sofía, Nico, Bernardo, and baby Max.

Joining the Entrepreneurship Revolution

CHAPTER 13

Intrapreneurship

Steven D. Strauss

Senior small business columnist for USA Today, president of TheSelfEmployed.com, and top-selling author, Steve Strauss is often called "America's leading small business expert."

> Innovation has nothing to do with how many R&D dollars you have. When Apple came up with the Mac, IBM was spending at least 100 times more on R&D. It's not about money. It's about the people you have, how you're led, and how much you get it.
>
> —Steve Jobs

*W*e have all heard that old Chinese proverb: *"May you live in interesting times." Well, these are interesting times for sure, very interesting. The world is changing before us—physically, politically, and economically. The Arab Spring is yet unfolding. Social media allows for the instantaneous direct dissemination of ferment and ideas. Climate change changes everything.*

How will we navigate these changes? Throughout this book, various authors have shared the idea that thinking and acting "entrepreneurially" is key, and while that does mean "taking a risk with money to make money," it also means much more. It requires nothing less than thinking creatively, inspiring innovation, seeing problems, and taking smart, calculated risks to solve them. It requires vision and forethought and bravery and self-reliance and initiative and boldness. It requires entrepreneurship in all of its forms.

So whether you want to create a business that is more entrepreneurial, a social enterprise that can be self-sufficient while tackling The Big Problem, or a revolution to overthrow a dictator, you will need to foster entrepreneurship within your ranks. By bringing out the entrepreneurial spirit in your people, you tap into their better angels, their creative power, their idealism and realism, and together, you all join the ranks of Planet Entrepreneur.

■ ■ ■

Entrepreneurs tend to start out as lone wolves—they come up with some zany idea on a walk or in a garage or on the treadmill or skydiving or whatever. But then—very rapidly, and if they are good—these entrepreneurs become part of a pack. They somehow enlist enough people in that vision to make the dream become a reality. Great entrepreneurs bring out the best in themselves and their team.

When you empower people to think and act entrepreneurially within your business or organization, it is called "intrapreneurship." Intrapreneurship is all about encouraging employees to think, dream, act, and create as though they were entrepreneurs themselves. It might be an employee who comes up with a great idea or a staffer in a social enterprise who sees a powerful new way to move the cause forward. Either way, it's internal entrepreneurship, intrapreneurship.

How do you do that, how do you get people to act intrapreneurially? It requires doing many things right, including:

- Giving incentives
- Creating an entrepreneurial culture
- Rewarding, and not penalizing, risk-taking

An intrapreneur is an employee who is given freedom and financial support to create new products, services and systems, who does not have to follow the company's usual routines or protocols.[1]

—Sir Richard Branson in *Entrepreneur* magazine

---

[1] www.entrepreneur.com/article/218011.

That last point is critical. You cannot create a culture of intra-preneurship if employees are not expected to innovate, are not motivated to innovate, and are not rewarded for innovating. To have a thriving culture of intrapreneurship, a business must not only invite innovation, it must reward risk-taking as well.

Why Should Your Business Be Thinking about Intrapreneurship?

Many forward-thinking corporations now are welcoming and encour-aging their employees to make innovative and thoughtful entrepreneurial contributions. Gifford Pinchot, who first made the term intrapreneurship popular in his 1985 book, *Intrapreneuring*, wrote, "Look back at any great business or invention at just about any big company and you can find that intrapreneurs created it." This statement sums up why any company looking to effectively prosper and advance in today's business climate should be thinking about providing the time, resources, culture, and encouragement that fosters intrapreneurship.

The Intraprenurial Culture

When companies set up an intrapreneurial environment, an environment that encourages risk-taking and innovation, they benefit in very tangible ways. For starters, they will likely see a rise in the reliability, happiness, diligence, and productivity of their employees. Employees become more enthusiastic in general when they are able to work on projects that are:

- Personally fulfilling
- Financially rewarding
- Capable of making a difference

This enthusiasm will carry over to their work in general.

Corporations have also found that encouraging intrapreneurship is an effective tactic when it comes to attracting and keeping the best talent. When employees can act creatively, explore their ideas, and have a chance to succeed and prosper with these concepts, they experience higher levels of job satisfaction. Ultimately, intrapreneurship then increases employee retention rates, boosts productivity, and fosters an exceptional culture.

Back in the mid-1980s, Coca-Cola was the world's number-one soft drink maker, but Pepsi was coming on strong: Between "The Pepsi Challenge" TV commercials and the endorsement deal with pop star Michael Jackson, Pepsi looked to be young, hip, and "the choice of a new generation," while Coke seemed old and a bit stodgy.

Afraid of losing both their mojo and market share, executives at Coca-Cola decided to secretly create a soda that could rival Pepsi. After months of secretly tinkering and testing, they had it: New Coke. Convinced they had a winner, the Coca-Cola people decided to throw away one of the oldest, best-known and most beloved brands on the planet—Coke. It was a complete and utter disaster. New Coke became an instant punch line, was uniformly derided, people wanted to hate it, and it was off store shelves within three months.

And the executives who took this chance, they all got fired, right? Wrong. Not by a long shot; in fact, they were all promoted. Even though the experiment failed, upper management loved the bold risk-taking that the initiative required.

Now that is an intrapreneurial culture.

In Richard Branson's column in *Entrepreneur* magazine quoted above, he described how Virgin has always encouraged intrapreneurs. This model allowed for many opportunities within his company that translated to success for employees and the growth of Virgin. He relayed a story that took place back when Virgin Airlines was looking to design the upper class cabin. They were seeking an innovative solution, but, as it turned out, they couldn't find any seat design firms able to pull off their needs according to the specifications. A young designer who worked at Virgin insisted that he wanted to give it a shot. Instead of shooing him away in favor of those well-respected design firms, Virgin allowed him to try. And unlike the more seasoned designers that had tried their hand at the project and failed, this young designer offered truly out-of-the-box thinking and creativity. The end result of his efforts was the creation of "horizontal fliers," which turned out to be very attractive to customers and became a signature offering at Virgin Airlines. Intrapreneurship to the rescue!

Branson also explained that when Virgin began their mobile phone division, they were new to the niche. So to get up to speed quickly,

Virgin hired top managers from rival companies and then gave them the freedom to set up internal ventures of their own. This intraprenurial process resulted in innovative thinking and a very profitable new business: Virgin Mobile. Branson writes, "What if CEO stood for 'chief enabling officer'? What if that CEO's primary role were to nurture a breed of intrapreneurs who would grow into tomorrow's entrepreneurs?"

The key here for companies is to create a structure that allows employees to pursue their visions. Their employees' success will quickly become their success.

Example: The Minnesota Mining & Manufacturing Company, also known as 3M, is another company that historically has valued and encouraged innovation and intrapreneurship. Not only do they allow technical employees to spend 15 percent of their time working on projects of their own choosing, but the company as a whole stresses a spirit of innovation, risk-taking, and collaboration.

In 1968, a research scientist at 3M invented a new substance quite by accident when he experimented with various solutions in an attempt to improve the adhesive that 3M used in some of their tapes. The substance he accidentally invented was an adhesive that didn't really stick to anything very well. However, this new substance remained sticky even after you changed its location various times. The perplexed scientist brainstormed and talked to colleagues at 3M about this gummy substance, but no one knew what to do with it. He was even given the opportunity to host some seminars within the company discussing what he had discovered. One of the employees that attended one of his seminars was a development researcher named Art Fry.

Fry was very intrigued by the gluey substance, but also did not know what to do with it on a practical level. Then, one day, a long time later, he was singing in the choir at his church. He had placed little pieces of paper to mark his place in the hymnal, but they kept falling out. He thought to himself that what he truly needed was a sticky bookmark.

Eureka!

Suddenly, Fry put two and two together and realized that the mystery adhesive his friend had invented would work perfectly for this purpose. Then, only after writing a note on one of these sticky bookmarks and affixing it to a report did Fry come "to the very exciting realization that my sticky bookmark was actually a new way to communicate and organize information." The end result of this inventor's innovative thinking was the Post-it note. As they say, the rest was history: Post-its were named as one of the top consumer products of the decade. And it all happened because 3M had created a culture that valued such intrapreneurial, collaborative thinking.

What Intraprenurial Companies Do Right

Clearly, 3M and Virgin have been on the forefront of the intrapreneurial movement for many years. But there are many other companies around the world that have also embraced this strategy and used it to their advantage.

> Dr. Howard Edward Haller, in his book *Intrapreneurship Success*, writes, "Innovation and intrapreneurship are the 'secret weapon' for success within major firms such as 3M, Anaconda-Ericsson, Apple Computer, Autodesk, Corona Data Systems, Caribou Coffee, Gateway, GE, Genentech, Google, IBM, INTEL, iRobot, Kodak, Lockheed-Martin, PR1ME Computer, Sony, Sun Microsystems, TCI, Texas Instruments, Toyota, W. L. Gore, and Yahoo."

Similar to 3M, Google gives not only engineers, but all employees, 20 percent free time to work on projects of their own choosing. Employees are encouraged to come up with new ideas that benefit the company. Intrapreneurs at Google are encouraged to discuss their ideas and get creative input from their coworkers. This process lets their concepts get tossed around a bit, and through this process, ideas get fine-tuned and become better and better.

After the refinement by the crowd, there is a formal review process set up at Google. A project proposal and timeline needs to be submitted. The intrapreneur must describe how he or she plans to go about evaluating the success of the project. Once an outstanding project has been selected, there is a set process through which a project is effectively monitored. According to Marissa Mayer, former Vice President of Search Products and User Experience at Google, half of all new products created at Google originated from this process. Gmail, AdSense, and Orkut were all started by Intraprenurial employees. Google is constantly launching internal mini start-ups and it goes without saying that many are quite successful.

There are a number of reasons why the strategy described above works for large companies like Google. First of all, it avoids the slow process of clearing new ideas with various levels of management and corporate boards. Secondly, Google also gives people credit. They consistently give praise to people who take risks and actually make it cool to do so, even if their ideas are not successful. After all, how else can you get better? Trying and failing is a vital part of the process.

Another important factor depends on encouraging employees to think out of the box; that means that their ideas don't necessarily have to relate to the core business. For example, Intel came up with an initiative back in 1998 that encouraged new ideas from employees even if they didn't have to do with their main business of making chips. Intel soon began to actually finance new businesses started by employees as they had realized that many of their best employees were busy doing entrepreneurial endeavors outside of work. By welcoming their ideas at the workplace, they figured out a way to retain that creative energy and put it to work on behalf of the company.

Global Intrapreneurship

Corporations in other countries, of course, haven't neglected the power of creating an intrapreneurial culture. The Canadian design, entertainment software, and engineering company Autodesk created "Autodesk Ventures" back in the mid-1990s. This division began to invest in start-ups and incubate new business. In 1999, employees created a website called Buzzsaw, which was a collaborative design tool for the construction industry. Autodesk incubated the idea and then the company spun off Buzzsaw.com. Quickly, $90 million was raised in venture capital. Autodesk got some very positive recognition from this project, and their stock price dramatically increased.

The Innovation in Japan–U.S. Business and Technology Awards program now gives out an annual Intrapreneur–Japan award. Last year, the winner was the East Japan Railway Company for its intrapreneur who came up with the "Suica paperless ticketing and payment services system." Recently, the system became available for smart phones, and this development has completely transformed and updated public transportation in Japan.

Projects that employees are passionate about often will reflect social issues they feel strongly about. As a result, in a successful intrapreneurial climate, many projects have a social and environmental slant. One good example of this is the launch of Opal fuel at BP Australia. BP Australia worker Mark Glazebrook discovered that "petrol sniffing" was becoming an epidemic in the indigenous communities. Various fuel companies throughout the company were being urgently alerted to this deadly issue. Glazebrook told his BP corporate execs that he would like to help solve the problem. He was encouraged to do so, and took a trip to find out more. Glazebrook visited the communities and talked to the local governments, kids, and elders. He found out that one key issue leading to the problem was that communities had no control over the kind of fuel they received. Glazebrook realized that if he could get BP to develop a low vapor fuel, indigenous people could no longer get a "high" from the fuel. Thus, Opal fuel was launched.

This new fuel has become extremely successful throughout Australia. Canada is now even importing it to deal with fuel sniffing in their indigenous communities. Through his intrapreneurial endeavors, not only was Glazebrook able to create a successful product, but he also helped save lives in the process.

Tips for Fostering Intrapreneurs

Intrapreneurship can be stressful for employees, especially when they are taking a creative leap without knowing whether or not they will be successful. They have their own reputation, and that of their employer, to consider. While their successes will be widely acknowledged, the inverse holds true as well. That means that if their ideas fail, they will also be responsible. Employees have a position to uphold. No one wants to take a risk, even with the best of intentions, and then end up losing their job, so the intrapreneurial enterprise will make it easy and safe for staffers to take calculated risks.

Here are a five ways to do that:

1. **Share the equity.** If you really want to promote intrapreneurship, you might want to consider giving all employees an ownership stake in the business. When employees own even a few shares of the business, they:

- Become very invested in the success of the company
- Become more entrepreneur than employee
- Think of work as something more than just a place to draw a salary

Studies show that employees who have a financial stake in the business are more conscientious, harder working, and happier. They will likely be even more passionate about the project that they have launched and more motivated to ensure it is successful.

Depending on the type of business you have, there are many different ways to cut the equity pie, but whatever way an owner chooses, it is true that he or she will be giving up part of their equity in the business to create the employee ownership plan. The benefit, of course, is that they would be able to attract the best and the brightest of employees and create an incredibly motivated, dedicated workforce in the process, which helps create an even bigger and better business.

2. **Give people a green light.** Providing employees with the time and resources they need is crucial, but they also must believe that they can successfully navigate through your company's formalities. Often those with intrapreneurial leanings are afraid to try out their ideas because they anticipate too many roadblocks. Employees need to know that they will have a level of autonomy and that middle and senior management will be receptive to ideas. When an employee shares their big idea and plans, managers must listen.

So you have to keep the pipeline open to new ideas. If possible, go ahead and streamline your system so that you encourage employees to share their best ideas. After all, who knows various facets of a company better than the employees? They likely see things about the inner workings of the company that those in management may easily overlook. As a result, employees are the perfect people to draw on for ideas for improvements and innovations.

3. **Have fun.** Anything that can be done in the spirit of fun can reap big rewards. Creative thinking workshops or classes can get employees' juices flowing. Some companies use a suggestion box and offer a prize to those who come up with the best ideas. Encourage those people from other departments to work together to come up with concepts and plans.

4. **Recognize them.** When good ideas are generated, it is important to follow up. Employees should see that their ideas are valued and being acted upon. A company looking to encourage intrapreneurship

should try to implement all great ideas and give credit where credit is due.

5. **Reward them financially.** Nothing talks like money. If you want your people to act entrepreneurially, then reward them accordingly.

Top 10 Ways to Create an Intraprenurial Organization

The "world's most popular innovation website" is InnovationExcellence .com. In a recent article (January 23, 2013), they listed the most important things the top companies do that create an exceptional Intraprenurial culture. Here is our Top 10:

1. **Look for it.** "Building an intrapreneurial culture isn't about 'creating' intrapreneurs; invariably they already exist within the organization, they just need to be discovered, nurtured, and loved."

2. **Be inclusive.** "An intrapreneurial culture builds value across the workforce, which is predicated upon giving people a voice in their own work."

3. **Give people ownership.** "To create an intrapreneurial culture, people must be empowered to make decisions—empowered to have ownership. In this respect, employees need to be encouraged to create solutions independently of the chain of command."

4. **Make risk-taking okay.** "As intrapreneurs make decisions, they must be willing to take intelligent risks and, although fully prepared to be held accountable, not fear persecution or ridicule if they fail."

5. **Include all employees.** "DreamWorks, a famously inclusive and intraprenurial business, encourages creativity from all its employees, even support staff such as accountants and lawyers. According to Dan Satterthwaite, Head of Human Resources, they actively solicit ideas and regularly receive hundreds from staff across the business."

6. **Offer room to play around.** "A practiced method for promoting intrapreneurship is to give individuals allocated time away from their 'day jobs' in order to encourage their creative processes."

7. **Celebrate and reward intrapreneurial behavior.** "Celebrate intrapreneurial successes and the people behind them—whether individuals or teams. Recognition and reward will act as significant affirmations for the intrapreneur and provide them with reasons to stay, continue to add value, and grow their contributions in the future."

8. **Encourage collaboration.** "A great misconception of intrapreneurship is that it is an individual sport. For any intrapreneurial venture to succeed, collaboration is required."

9. **Get to "yes" quickly.** "By shortening or circumventing the [process of getting to yes], companies can be more reactive to opportunities; drive innovation by activating a constant stream of ideas; and create a broad intrapreneurial culture leading to more engaged and empowered employees."

10. **Create and allocate a funding pot for intrapreneurial initiatives.** "One of the biggest hurdles for intrapreneurial ventures is the inability to secure the necessary resources, at the right time, in order to move the project forward. By carving out a funding pool specifically to be used to seed intrapreneurs, companies can enable greater traction for new ideas and thus increase the likelihood of creating new, sustainable business streams."

It is rare for companies to be able to hang onto their best talent. Yet, organizations (and not just businesses) that foster intrapreneurship have a distinct advantage. By encouraging staff to be innovative within the workplace, by giving them the tools, resources, and recognition that makes playing in this arena worthwhile, innovative, intrapreneurial organizations reap numerous benefits, including, and especially, a highly engaged workforce, and better products and services to sell.

Intrapreneurship is a powerful way to tap into, and get the best out of, your staff and your business. With it, you not only create a highly engaged workforce, but you will help foster the best in your business, and create some incredible products and services as a result. That is the power of intrapreneurship.

■ ■ ■

The senior *USA Today* small business columnist and top-selling author, **Steve Strauss**, is also a spokes-person for corporations wishing to tap the small business marketplace, a recovering lawyer, and a frequent media guest on TV and radio. He sits on the advisory board of the World Entrepreneurship Forum and regularly speaks across the globe about entrepreneurial business strategies and global trends in business.

Steve's company, The Strauss Group, creates cutting-edge business content for everyone from Fortune 100 companies to the *Huffington Post*, small chambers of commerce, and many others. His latest venture is the tech start-up TheSelfEmployed.com.

You can reach Steve at sstrauss@mrallbiz.com.

CHAPTER 14

Taking Your Business Global in the Digital Age

Laurel Delaney

Laurel Delaney is a successful entrepreneur, speaker, educator, and author with more than 25 years of global business experience. She runs Chicago-based GlobeTrade.com (a Global TradeSource, Ltd. company), a leading management, consulting, and marketing solutions company dedicated to helping entrepreneurs and small businesses go global.

> No nation was ever ruined by trade.
> —Benjamin Franklin (1706–1790),
> U.S. politician, inventor, and journalist

So by now you get it. The entrepreneurial global revolution is real, it's big, it's here to stay, and it's likely a trend of which you want to be a part. If you work in a large corporation, the previous chapter should have given you plenty of ideas, and if you are a solo entrepreneur, the next chapter is the one for you. For the regular small or medium business (SME) that wants to know how to know more about getting in on the action, this is the place for you. Pull up a chair, because it's time now to go global.

■ ■ ■

Consider these two facts: (1) The Internet is the world's meeting place. Today, more than 34 percent of the world's population is connected to the Internet, just about 2.5 billion people, and the numbers are growing every day. (2) As we have seen, entrepreneurs are, and will continue to be, a major driving force behind the world's economic growth. If we connect the dots, what is abundantly clear then is that using the Internet to take your business global is smart. And the good news is that in this e-era, it isn't that hard to do. So consider this your primer for taking your business global—fast!

The Everything Guide to Going Global

Going global is a logical process with multiple steps. Here's the first one:

Step 1: Do your research. Your first step to going global is to pick a product or service to take or source overseas. You can't be all things to all people nor should you be (or even want to be.) Decide on one thing. Then stick with it. Whether you are exporting a product, offering a service, or looking to import a product made to your specifications, *focus* is essential to getting it done right and timely.

> If you are looking to source a product, try Global Sources, ThomasNet, and Alibaba.

Once you have determined who you are going to buy from or sell to in the global marketplace, you need to decide how much you can afford to invest in your international expansion efforts. Will it be based on 10 percent of your domestic business profits, a fixed dollar amount—say $50,000 for the first year—a pay-as-you-can-afford process, or gut instincts? Early on, you must prepare financially, emotionally, and intellectually to go global.

The next piece of research you must undertake is market research. Up front, you need to identify your prime target markets; this is critical to the success of your venture. You may want to find out where your product will be in greatest demand. Market research is a powerful tool for exploring and identifying the fastest growing, most penetrable market for your product. As you research, pay close attention to any cultural differences in foreign markets and be ready to address them. And here is a tip you should definitely keep in mind: I always suggest you enter markets where you speak the language first. It makes things so much easier (as you will see in the rest of this chapter.)

To research international business intelligence, check out PIERS, Datamyne, and Import Genius.

Use this market research to predict how your product will sell in a specific geographic location. This will enable you to find out how much you will be able to sell over a specific period of time. Also, so as to better understand the context of what you are learning, be sure to check with your government to see what programs they have in place to help you analyze research data. For example, in the United States, we have Export .gov and the International Trade Administration. Wherever you are located, consulting companies, universities, small business development centers, government programs, and business intelligence organizations can all assist in the analysis (check out GlobeTrade, KPMG France, EMYLON Business School, and Nanyang Technological University, for example).

Step 2: Get your e-presence ready. To get your nascent global brand off of the ground, you *must* have a strong e-presence. Period. This starts with creating a website and a blog. If you want to own your online brand identity, build a broader global base, and move sales internationally, you better get a website and blog sooner rather than later. How else will international customers and suppliers find you?

It cannot be understated just how important your site and blog are. If you want potential customers to find you, if you want to be taken seriously, and if you want to become an international business, then a great site and blog are critical. Your site and blog must:

• Be professional, intuitive, and well designed
• Offer quality content that relates to your business and industry
• Be updated frequently

Note: Be sure to state what your goals are on your website. For example, if you want to do business with and from Brazil, say so, and provide an area where consumers or businesses in Brazil can click to communicate with you quickly. If you are seeking international distributors, spell it out.

These are places to look for help setting up a website: Network Solutions, Go Daddy, and WordPress. For a blog, try Blogger, WordPress, and Typepad.

An online presence is a great place to start, but beyond that you've got to ensure that people can find you on the Web, and that means that you must optimize your website and blog with keywords. Always keep search engine optimization (SEO) in the forefront when establishing new online platforms. Place keywords—words that define what you do—-strategically throughout your content. Having keyword-rich content is critical to performing well with search engines. Load your homepage and other critical pages with important keywords too. Keywords for my company, GlobeTrade, include "global small business, "going global," and "expand internationally." What are yours?

Focus on keywords that register well with search engines. How do you know what those words and phrases are? Don't guess. Instead, use a Keyword Analyzer Tool (Google the phrase and you will find many from which to choose.) Then type in what you think your keywords are and the tool will analyze those, and thousands of others. This will tell you what words are searched most often and therefore which are most important to have on your site. Embed these keywords in your anchor text used to describe links, your domain name, your page title, and your meta tags and use them in articles and blogs that you post on your site. Basic search engine optimization is fundamental and essential if you want to position your website properly and be found—especially when consumers want to buy!

So, now you have a website. Good. Have you attracted any interest from overseas customers? No? Then you need to turn your website into a global e-commerce money-making machine. To accomplish that, focus on three key areas:

1. **Language:** If you wish to expand your business internationally, say to Brazil and Spain, you'd better adapt your site to accommodate Portuguese- and Spanish-speaking visitors. Customers won't stay long on your site if they cannot understand the language you use.

2. **Online platform:** Let's say I am located in Australia and wish to buy 10,000 widgets from your website based in India. How do you make it easy for me to do business with your company? Can I put 10,000 units in the order quantity box on your site, click a button, and wait for my goods to arrive? The whole point of a great global e-commerce site is to make the visitor experience feel like it's local! Think Amazon, eBay, and Barnes & Noble. Follow the leaders.

   Next, to guarantee success, install an appropriate online e-commerce platform that can automatically detect who your visitors are and where they are located. This, in turn, will trigger automatic adjustments that are specifically tailored to the visitor concerning the international payment process (including a currency converter), global logistics, and even trade compliance, to name just a few.

3. **Customer service:** What happens when visitors click on the "Contact Us" button on your site? Will they get assistance in their language

A couple of e-commerce platforms to explore include Borderfree Global eCommerce, Shopify, Vine Global Solutions, and Digital River.

in a reasonable amount of time? How about "Live help"? Is it live, is there help, and is it in their language? For every minute a visitor waits to receive assistance from you at your website, it's a minute they're free to look elsewhere for the same offering. In many instances, they don't wait.

Website features and functions such as language translation, the e-commerce platform, and good customer service matters a lot to international shoppers. The ultimate goal is to drive online global sales to your business and at the same time make it easy for shoppers to browse, buy, and return to your website often.

Do You Need a Mobile Website?

Yes.

You need to establish a seamless, transactional mobile website that serves the world and delivers a healthy return on investment

(ROI). ABI Research predicts that $119 billion in goods and services will be purchased globally via mobile phones in 2015, representing about 8 percent of the total e-commerce market. What does this mean for you and your global business? Understand your global customer and determine how best to serve their needs on the go.

So the next step in your climb up the global business success ladder is to convert your website into a mobile-friendly site (e.g., dotMobi). This will engage individuals and drive participation to your company. Most blog platforms have a built-in mechanism to mobilize your blog; check with your host. And all the major social platforms automatically convert sites in a seamless manner from PC to mobile devices without users noticing any difference.

Whatever you communicate via global mobile, keep it short, sweet, and to the point. Frequency of messages matters, too. Mobile requires a completely different mindset. Convenience is crucial. Time is short. Attention span is even shorter. Emotions and responses are in real time, so you better get to your point or solution fast! And don't forget to give consumers a call to action.

Mobile users want information when they want it. In other words, they want to be in control of how and when they interact with a brand. If possible, personalize your message, which means getting to know your customers. This shows you care enough to give your best and are willing to target their specific needs. Intimacy or personalization through a mobile phone message plays a huge role in the direction the interaction takes.

Mobile commerce, or m-commerce, is commerce conducted using a mobile smart phone, tablet, tablet PC, or any other emerging Internet-enabled technology device that supports a seamless on-the-go consumer experience. In the future, it will redefine the way business is done all over the world, so start thinking about how to leverage this concept now to sell more stuff.

The Social Network

Needless to say, today, having a website, blog, and mobile version of your site is not enough. What's missing from that list in today's 24/7, connected, e-conomy? You know—social. Set up accounts with Facebook, LinkedIn, Twitter, Google+, Pinterest, and Instagram. The coolest aspect of the Internet is that it has no borders. Conversations can take place everywhere. So be sure to check out all of the different online social platforms and figure out which is (or which are) best for your business. Personally, LinkedIn is one in particular that I use most for making professional global connections, asking questions, and getting answers to international trade-related issues. But all of the different social networking sites have different strengths, so figure out which is best for your and your business and customers.

You need to position yourself properly on relevant networks and get noticed. That means talking up your business and your specific knowledge in a conversational way that engages people, educates them on something they don't already know, and motivates them to keep coming back to you for more. So tweet away, post valuable content on your Facebook page, and join specialized LinkedIn groups (for example, if you are already a member of the World Entrepreneurship Forum, join its LinkedIn group, or try the International Export Import [IEI] group or the International Business group, to name just a few).

Understanding Your New Market

Your next step is to establish a strategy that points to a direct or indirect method of going global. Once you have many options within your reach for getting your product into overseas markets, you can decide whether a direct or indirect (through an export intermediary) sales strategy will best serve your needs.

Step 3: Get globally ready. Getting globally ready boils down to an import or export strategy and how much control you wish to exercise over your activities. Regardless of whether you are selling direct or indirect, your customers will tend to fall into five categories:

1. Overseas agent or representative (importer)
2. Distributor or importing wholesaler
3. Overseas retailer
4. Overseas end user
5. Trading company

However you move your product, it's important to be aware of how many intermediaries will be involved in getting it to your consumers. Each one must add their markup to the price of your product in order to earn its due profit. Take this into consideration when you price your product, so that it won't end up being excessively expensive by the time it actually hits store shelves overseas. The most attractive import won't be able to compete with local products if it costs more than a consumer is willing to pay!

Now that you have your strategy in place, it is time to figure out how to adapt your products to a foreign marketplace. Many entrepreneurs, business owners, and executives believe it's only packaging (see "Japan Case Study") that has to be adapted in an overseas marketplace. Wrong. Many other factors are at play as well, such as the name of your brand, electrical power systems, weight and measures, ingredients in a product, physical environment, and so forth. Be sensitive about adapting your products and services to accommodate the global marketplace.

JAPAN CASE STUDY:
GIVE CUSTOMERS WHAT THEY WANT

Years ago I had a client who manufactured ice cream. Whether winter or summer, it flew out of supermarket freezers in the United States. Demand was so great domestically that the company knew its next big growth opportunity would be international expansion.

The company settled on Japan—a country exacting about quality—as the overseas entry point. Starting with a small test shipment and high hopes, the company quickly fell flat on its face. The first problem was that the company packed the ice cream in gallon containers, convenient for Americans' big freezers but a problem for Japanese preferences for everything small, especially appliances and individual products. The second problem was with the ice cream itself. The Japanese like their sweets far less sugary than Americans do.

If my client wanted to succeed in Japan, it would have to adapt its products to meet the needs of the Japanese marketplace. Trying again, the client packaged a reduced-sugar ice cream in individual-sized containers, shipping a 20-foot freezer container the first month. That one freezer grew to nearly 10 a month during the ensuing years. Had the company not made the change, had it not listened to the market, it would have had no business, literally or figuratively, in Japan.

When it is not possible to sell the standardized products and services, as in the ice cream producer's case, a small business must adapt if it wants to be a global business. And although the changes might be to satisfy foreign countries' regulatory requirements, the biggest test is always with the market—the customer—because that's who ultimately buys your product or service. If customers are not interested at your offering, even with regulatory approval, there will be no sales. Always keep the customer top of mind and have empathy for another's point of view; it will lead to ideas for understanding and dealing with cultural differences.

Logistics and Payments

Now that you've designed your product with a foreign buyer in mind, the next step is to work on the logistics of actually getting that product or service into your customer's hands. That starts with preparing pricing and determining *landed costs*. Landed costs include the original price of the product, all transportation fees (both inland and ocean), customs, duties, taxes, insurance, currency conversion, crating, handling, and payment fees.

Be ready to test out your price on your customer. And then negotiate from there. Prepare what is called a pro forma invoice, showing all the familiar components of an ordinary domestic invoice: a description of the product, an itemized listing of charges, and sales terms. And then determine a landed cost, which is the total price of a product once it has arrived at a buyer's door. I emphasize the landed cost model because that way, you maintain control over your profits and the buyer knows exactly what his costs and profits will be as well. Everyone wins.

Set up terms, conditions, and other financing options. One of the most important things to negotiate before closing on a global sale is how payment will be made. Short of asking for payment in advance, securing payment with a letter of credit is the next best option. Yes, it's a little more expensive—typically one eighth of a percent of the total transaction price plus incidental fees related to any amendments that might have to be made—but it's worth it to know you have a secure method of payment. There's no price tag for peace of mind. Enlist your banker to assist with best options for financing an international sale.

Other payment options are wire transfer of funds, documentary collections (a sight draft, for example), and open account (this is where neither a buyer or seller knows how payment will be collected and is especially a bad idea for a new customer). With technology, there are additional ways to collect money from overseas: PayPal, Square, Intuit

GoPayment, and Google Wallet. Many big banks are now offering payment devices to easily accept credit cards from all over the world. Most of the online payment vehicles charge a fee for conducting the transaction (anywhere from 2.75 to 3.5 percent plus, in some cases, a per-transaction fee).

"Many young exporting companies fear how to either get paid for or finance their transactions. One thing that American exporters should look into is the SBA's pre-export line of credit, which has several variations," says Tess Morrison, former director of the International Trade Center at the University of Illinois, Urbana-Champaign. "The government will guarantee to your bank 90 percent of the loaned amount. You can then borrow against an international order to fulfill that order." Check with the nearest international SBA office or your state's international trade office for help with the application paperwork. Readers who reside outside the United States should check with their government to see what international trade programs are in place to foster exports.

Next, brush up on documentation and legal regulatory procedures. Hire a freight forwarder or a logistics expert such as UPS, FedEx, DHL, or TNT to help you with paperwork because you have to get it right. These companies are experts at moving cargo from anywhere in the world by surface (which includes the ocean) and air carriers. Use their expertise to your advantage. You will want to find out what documentation is required to move your product from one country to another, who prepares it, how long it takes, and what bumps you might anticipate along the way. Each country has its own twists on taxes, rules, and regulations that suddenly become part of the cross-border experience.

International shipping: Shipping your goods abroad can be a challenge logistically: You need to understand how to pack your product without it breaking, as well as how to navigate the rules and regulations for each country. Additional costs that may come with engaging in cross-border commerce include, but are not limited to: brokerage and logistic fees, transport costs, customs duties, taxes, tariffs, special packing costs (if required), insurance (if needed), currency conversion, and handling fees. That is why it is best to search out and find a solid international shipping partner—someone with the experience to make your job easier. The right company will handle all of the logistics for you and make handling the administrative issues a breeze.

Next, be sure to hire a good lawyer, a savvy banker, a knowledgeable accountant, and a seasoned transport specialist, each of whom should specialize in international transactions. These people will be able to guide you in your financial and logistical decisions. You may feel that you can't afford these professional services, but in truth, you can't afford to do without them. One mistake can be very costly. Listen to their advice. Your team members should work in concert to keep your enterprise in the most advantageous legal and financial position possible.

Getting Customers

There is no business overseas for you unless you locate customers first, so now we then come to the last step.

Step 4: Find customers. Global success won't happen overnight. Plan at least a two-year lead-time for world market penetration. It takes time and patience to build a great, enduring global enterprise, so be patient and plan for the long haul. Sure, you'll get nibbles here and there from people visiting your website, blog, and social platforms, but real business takes time to develop. Anticipate a customer courtship that might run anywhere from three months to two years before you hit your stride. Once you do, the strength of your relationship will determine how much future business comes your way.

The solution, from a North American perspective, is to focus on a free resource such as the U.S. Commercial Service, which provides customized market research, general insights (including cultural insights), and market reports on various industries in almost any market in the world with export potential. "Most of our services are of little or no cost to companies," says my colleague and friend Mary Joyce, network director, U.S. Department of Commerce, Upper Midwest Export Assistance Centers. "One of our key services, the Gold Key, actually sets up appointments with potential buyers, agents, and distributors for a company, making a business trip for any size company much more efficient and cost-effective."

For folks outside the United States, check with your government, entrepreneurial centers, and small business incubators for help finding cross-border customers. Many have programs in place that help fosters exports in a country.

> Exhibiting at or attending a trade show or conference is a uniquely effective way to contact cross-border customers, especially if you have a difficult product to sell or a product that a customer needs to see in person. Exhibiting is powerful because it allows you to get your company name out there and have potential buyers meet you face to face. For example, the International Housewares Association has an exhibition in the United States and provides a number of benefits to help its members increase sales globally. Other industry associations offer similar assistance.

Provided you do your homework, trade shows can connect you with customers, suppliers, agents, and brokers—and allow you to generate new revenue and greater profitability for your business. Another way to expand your international customer base is to check out cross-border alliances and partnerships; consider joining forces with another company of similar size and market presence that is located in a foreign country where you are already doing business or would like to. "Identify a trusted and knowledgeable on-site person," says Dr. Ray Smilor, internationally recognized expert in entrepreneurship and Schumacher Fellow and Professor of Professional Practice at Neeley School of Business at Texas Christian University. "You might find this person—who has a good personal network, knows how to work in the domestic system, and can make introductions and connections for you—via references or previous experience."

Once you have identified some viable targets, make personal contact with them. Arm yourself with culture-specific information, courtesies, professionalism, and consistency. Your goal should be, when you enter a different culture, to learn it, adapt to it, and then make it your own. "Visit on a regular basis," Smilor says. Keep in mind, finding good and trustworthy people to have a great business relationship with is not easy.

Final Thoughts

Keep in mind a few final thoughts as you head out into international waters:

Build an app. Mobile apps are increasingly being used to boost productivity and automate businesses (Dropbox, Flipboard, Skype, Genius Scan, and Wi-Fi Finder, for example). The next wave of business mobility, fueled by smart phones and tablets, will deliver a real ROI through automation processes. Many businesses are replacing paper-based processes with mobile processes. What app can you build that will create value for your community of consumers and customers? What can you create that will generate a new source of mobile revenue and garner greater market share? The goal of your app is to take center stage on a user's smart phone home screen.

Use cloud computing to your advantage. Everybody is talking about the importance of the next new growth environment—cloud computing for entrepreneurs. But have you ever thought about it as a way to go global? This can be a strategic decision that helps you tackle the inherent small business problem of having limited resources.

Imagine this for your small business: You take all your HR data and place it in a private, company-owned cloud for 24/7 access. Employees use the cloud to streamline workflow and vastly improve how managers respond to challenges and opportunities, as well as employee questions and concerns. After monitoring, testing, and verifying the performance of the cloud, you realize you've saved an astounding amount in hardware, power, and IT support costs.

The "cloud" is simply a remote data center, controlled by a vendor, that you access via the Internet. You can share, edit, store, and play files on these remote servers. Google's Gmail, Apps, Docs, and Sites are all forms of cloud computing.

Laurel insight: Cloud computing will play a major role for global entrepreneurs and small business owners in application delivery. Someday, not too far off in the future, customers anywhere in the world with a mobile device will be able to text you their next big container order, and all you will have to do is hit four keystrokes—ASPD: Acknowledge, Ship, Pay, and Deliver. That's it. All of it will be pre programmed as a typical online process for an international sales transaction.

And finally, enjoy your global journey. Never forget that you are the most valuable business asset you have, and that the human touch is all the more precious in our age of high technology. Take the best possible care of yourself, your employees, and your customers, and your future will be bright, prosperous and happy.

Have I persuaded you to join the global revolution? By joining this revolution, you'll be in good company. And it just might spur your business to heights you never imagined.

Websites to Help You Go Global

About.com Import and EXPORT
    www.importexport.about.com
globalEDGE (from Michigan State University)
    http://globaledge.msu.edu
Global Reach Blog
    http://globalreach.blogs.census.gov
GlobeTrade
    www.globetrade.com
International Trade Administration, U.S. Department of Commerce
    www.ita.doc.gov/index.html
Office of International Trade, U.S. Small Business Administration
    www.sbaonline.sba.gov/index.html
The Federation of International Trade Associations
    www.fita.org/index.html
The U.S. government export portal
    www.export.gov
The Global Small Business Blog
    www.globalsmallbusinessblog.com

■ ■ ■

 **Laurel Delaney** runs Chicago-based GlobeTrade .com (a Global TradeSource, Ltd. company), a leading management consulting and marketing solutions company dedicated to helping entrepreneurs and small businesses go global. The United States Small Business Administration has recognized Ms. Delaney as a world-renowned global small business expert by naming her the "Illinois Exporter of the Year."

She is the author of "Start and Run a Profitable Exporting Business" and is the creator of a social media platform comprising of four blogs: Escape from Corporate America, Women Presidents' Organization Chicago Chapter, The Global Small Business Blog, and Women Entrepreneurs GROW Global. She is a charter member of the World Entrepreneurship Forum, serves as the Import/Export Guide for About.com and is the Chicago chapter chair for the Women Presidents' Organization.

Ms. Delaney holds an MBA from Lake Forest Graduate School of Management and is currently at work on a new book on exporting to be published February 2014 by Apress. You can reach Laurel at ldelaney@ globetrade.com.

CHAPTER 15

The Self-Employed Entrepreneur

Steven D. Strauss

Senior small business columnist for USA Today, *president of TheSelfEmployed.com, and top-selling author, Steve Strauss is often called "America's leading small business expert."*

> The credit belongs to the man who is actually in the arena, whose face is marred by dust and sweat and blood; who strives valiantly; who errs, who comes short again and again, because there is no effort without error and shortcoming; but who does actually strive to do the deeds; who knows great enthusiasms, the great devotions; who spends himself in a worthy cause; who at the best knows in the end the triumph of high achievement, and who at the worst, if he fails, at least fails while daring greatly.
>
> —U.S. President Teddy Roosevelt

*T*he global entrepreneurial revolution takes many forms. It is the green entrepreneur looking for a sustainable solution, the businessman looking to produce the next big thing, the social entrepreneur fighting poverty, and here, the solo entrepreneur, enabled by technology and fortitude, taking on the world. Ironically, while the self-employed may feel like they are alone, they are anything but. By far, the largest category of business on the planet is the solopreneur. In the United States, of the 28 million business entities, the largest category—making up *almost 20 of the 28 million—are the self-employed. The same is true in almost any country in the world. In Europe, almost 35 million people are classified as self-employed, accounting for almost 20 percent of total employment. And while the most recent global recession surely hit them hard, a European Commission study found that self-employed entrepreneurs tend to be much more able to withstand economic downturns than your typical employee.*

The self-employed: Small, but mighty.

And yet, like just about everything else that has been examined in this book, the business of the self-employed, the microbusiness, the solopreneur (call it what you will) is changing rapidly. Indeed, maybe more than any other category on Planet Entrepreneur, it is the self-employed business that is being transformed by technology today. Technology generally, and computers and the Internet specifically, are giving microbusinesses the tools to compete, be effective, be efficient and professional, to look every bit as big as a big business, and still be a viable, pliable small business.

A long time ago, in a galaxy far, far away, a self-employed individual was stuck. Stuck making a little money running a little business in their little area. Not so now. Today, self-employed entrepreneurs are taking over the planet. The playing field has been leveled, and it looks increasingly like the small shall inherit the Earth.

■ ■ ■

How much is the world changing? Consider this: According to a recent report issued by the software firm VMware, "the term 'employee' will probably disappear in the second half of the twenty-first century, as workers transition into becoming their own business."

> There are millions of people now that work when they want, where they want, and on projects for which they are passionate and energized. We know them as the self-employed, freelancers, independent contractors. But it is only the start. The increasingly outdated model of job postings, internal transfers, and employment agreements is disintegrating and is being replaced by a new [self-employment] work model of the future that has enormous implications for both the individual and the economy.
>
> —Fast Company, "Free Agent Nation"

The Changing Nature of Work

It is no secret that the nature of work is changing rapidly right now, significantly and for the better. How do we love thee? Let us count the ways:

- More people than ever are working outside of an office—when, where, and how they want
- Most employees, employers, and entrepreneurs have abandoned the traditional 9-to-5 workday
- Mobility rules the day
- And a whole new generation of workers is discovering that they don't need that job that they once thought was so indispensable

It's a mutiny, a self-employment insurgency.

Here is an example of one such extraordinary insurgent: AJ Leon decided that working in Manhattan for the big firm making the big bucks was a big waste of his time and talent. As he says, "I used to be an unremarkably average finance executive in New York with a six-figure salary." Then, on December 31, 2007, realizing that he was "living someone else's life," he up and quit to join the ranks of the self-employed. And he decided to do so in a uniquely radical way. Leon decided his business would have no home office, in fact, it would have no offices at all. Wanting to travel and do work that "makes a difference," AJ started the creative design business, Misfit. Now, several years later, he and his wife travel the world, work and run their business from the road, and have a virtual staff of nine who work from all corners of the globe.

Here is AJ's remarkable story, in his own words: "For many years, I lived the life I was supposed to live, you know, the one that your parents and your teachers and your friends think you should. I graduated from university Summa Cum Laude with three degrees, and accepted a job offer at the largest firm I could find, paying the highest salary I could get. I did what you do in finance and jumped from firm to firm, following the money and climbing the proverbial ladder.

"There was this small issue, though. Like many people, it was never the life I actually wanted. I was terrified—my life seemed to be sailing further away from who I really was. Then it struck me. I realized that if I didn't leave right there and then, I was going to be that dude for the rest of my life. For the first time in my life, it occurred to me that I didn't have to live the life I was supposed to live, I could live the one I was destined to live. I walked out. My very own emancipation.

"I created Misfit, Inc. on purpose to be a nomadic, creative shop. Anyone who understands what I am talking about can do something similar in his or her world. I believe I have something to say to a generation of Misfits like me that don't quite fit in the parameters that the world set out for them. People that are just inches away from remarkable, and only need to see that there is indeed another way."

Aside from changing attitudes and new tech tools, there are many other things that have coalesced to create this sort of work revolution that AJ Leon and his tribe are taking advantage of. A significant factor in the rise in self-employment is the New Economy. With global unemployment still unusually high, with employers increasingly hiring part time workers and contractors, many people have become "accidental entrepreneurs" out of necessity. Additionally, because corporations are concluding that they need not hire people at full-time hours for full-time wages and benefits any more, underemployment is becoming all too real. So this too is adding to the ranks of free agent nation.

Yet within this new matrix lies a new paradigm: The era of the self-employed, "micro-multinational" company is upon us. Entrepreneurship is becoming a preferred way to overcome unemployment, underemployment, stagnation, boredom, and obsolescence. It is the affordable option and the hot ticket, the new old way to break away, make a difference, fire your boss, and perhaps even get rich—all at once.

The Tide of History

This is, without a doubt, the greatest time in the history of the planet to start, own, run, and grow your own business. Hyperbole? No. Fact. The age of the self-employed is now. In the past generation, five different seminal events/factors/changes have combined to transform the world into one where the self-employed entrepreneur, the AJ Leons of the world, grow ever more dominant:

1. **New markets:** Between the rise of capitalism worldwide and the emergence of new e-markets, there are now millions more potential new customers available to the entrepreneur. Any self-employed individual can now be a global business—a revolutionary fact never before true in human history.

2. **Attitudes:** Because capitalism has proven to be the best economic system, and because entrepreneurs are now the new global rock stars, small business and entrepreneurship are now in vogue. And because of this, the idea of owning your own business, once a somewhat remote and exotic idea, is not only doable, it has become quite desirable—chic, even. The self-employed are on the march because, among other reasons, people now get that small business is smart business.

3. **Technology:** As indicated, this may be the most important reason, and biggest change, of all. The ways in which technology has fueled the entrepreneurial revolution has been discussed thoroughly throughout this book, but for the self-employed entrepreneur, the short list includes:
   - Powerful software that enables any microbusiness the same tools that were once the domain of only big business
   - Websites that allow the self-employed entrepreneur to look big
   - E-commerce, social media, laptops, tablets, and smartphones that allow the self-employed to work anywhere, anytime
   - Smart phones and apps that allow anyone, even the Bottom of the Pyramid, the ability to be connected and participate in the information age

4. **Help:** Small business people are no longer on their own. Today, there is an abundance of help out there: websites, NGOs, mentorship programs, software programs, and so on. Additionally, banks are lending again, crowdfunding is coming into its own, and other creative financial solutions are now available. Combined, this means that there is really a lot of institutional help available to the small business owner.

5. **History:** All of the preceding combined means that the tide of the present and the wave of the future are headed in the same direction: towards the ascendance and dominance of entrepreneurship and small business in the global marketplace.

Thus, what we are seeing, according to Ken Phillips, co-founder and Executive Director of Independent Contractors of Australia, is:

> . . . *a seismic shift in the way jobs are created and economic value added [in] a new type of company, the micro-multinational. Traditionally, these small, self-starting, service-driven companies would have been described as small- and medium-sized enterprises, or SMEs, but thanks to the Internet, the emergence of new business platforms, and the increased openness of the global economy, these companies can enter markets with a minimum of bureaucracy and overhead.*
>
> *Add to that their unparalleled ability to respond promptly to changing market developments, a collaborative DNA that often translates into superior innovation performance and the lack of the institutional inertia, and legacy relationships plaguing larger organizations, and one begins to see the transformative and paradigm-changing potential.*

And with this change in the way people are working, we are also seeing a corresponding shift in how they live. Cities, for the most part, are often designed based on the old way of working, with different districts being zoned as "residential" or "commercial." But what happens when residential and commercial become one, when people create businesses in their basement and work from home? What happens when their private life is the same as their work life and there is no bright line between the two because people now expect to work how they want, and often that means at home or at Starbucks? The rise of the entrepreneurial self-employed class is thus radically changing how we live, work, and organize our lives and homes.

Why Join the Revolution?

There are many very good reasons to become a self-employed entrepreneur, but consider this ironic one: *Self-employment offers greater job security than working for someone else.* As we all know only too well, bosses can fire you. But when you are self-employed, you should have a pretty good boss, and he or she won't fire you (although he or she may work you too hard, but that's a different issue). Sure, you may lose a client, but you can go get another one. When you are an employee, however, you have but one "client," and when that client lets you go, that's when the trouble begins.

Additionally, microbusinesses have many built-in advantages that bigger businesses simply do not have:

- The ability to respond more personally to clients and customers
- Being able to pivot and make course-corrections quickly
- General flexibility
- Having the team feel like family
- The trust factor—people tend to trust small businesses more than large corporations

So yes, small business advantages are valuable and real, and the cool part today is that while the small business can look and act big, the big business can't really act small; that is, corporations inherently are not as responsive and personal as the microbusiness. So chalk another one up for the little guy.

A great place to start your entreprenurial journey is TheSelf Employed .com, where you will find articles, video, podcasts, special deals—everything you need to make your journey a fruitful and fun one.

Other reasons to consider self-employment are:

- The chance to be your own boss, make your own decisions, and live and work on your own terms
- The potential to make more money
- The chance to be more creative
- The ability to build equity in a business
- The chance to make a difference

Get Started

All of this prompts the question: How exactly do you do it, how do you join the ranks of the self-employed—especially when you have a job and responsibilities?

Successful self-employment requires many things, including vision, creativity, tenacity, the ability to handle ambiguity, hard work, and yes, that all important consideration and factor, passion. Let's consider business passion in a little more detail. It is often said that passion is the secret ingredient when it comes to business success. That is, and is not, true. Yes, passion is what sees you through the hard times, but it is equally true that passion doesn't pay the bills. Having a good plan, a business that serves the market, and efficient execution are probably just as important as passion in the entrepreneurial equation.

That said, the way most people become an entrepreneur is this: They fall in love. They fall in love with an idea—either for a specific business or more generally, with the idea of becoming an entrepreneur—and like any big love, it won't let go. They can't not do it. After that, there are many steps that go into taking an idea, executing on it, making a profit, and keeping it going, but that is for another day and another book. The important thing to know is that the first step is this: Becoming an entrepreneur means taking a risk. You must risk challenging the conventional with the unconventional, and you do that by seeing a problem and deciding to fix it—whatever that problem may be.

The advantage that the individual has over big corporations and big governments is that he or she needs no permission to take the initiative and become more entrepreneurial in their thinking and actions. Consider the wise words of the once and great futurist, Buckminster Fuller. He was, he decided one day, a "trim tab":

> *Something hit me very hard once, thinking about what one little man could do. Think of the Queen Mary—the whole ship goes by and then comes the rudder. And there's a tiny thing at the edge of the rudder called a trim tab. It's a miniature rudder. Just moving the little trim tab builds a low pressure that pulls the rudder around. Takes almost no effort at all. So I said that the little individual can be a trim tab. So I said, call me Trim Tab.*

According to *The Daily Telegraph*, Great Britain recorded the highest number of the self-employed ever in 2012. "Howard Archer, chief U.K. and European economist, said that the record level of self-employed people shows that thousands of Britons are "not very confident" about getting a job. "People think that their best chance is setting up for themselves," he said.

The tiny trim tab turns the rudder, and the little rudder turns the bigger ocean liner. Before long, that giant ocean liner is heading in a new direction, all because that tiny trim tab set things upon a new course.

The self-employed entrepreneur is the trim tab of today.

In the end, that is the true essence of this entrepreneurial revolution of which we speak. This world can be a challenging place, full of pessimism, violence, and obstruction. And yet there is also a tremendous push towards making it freer, cleaner, more sustainable, and more prosperous. You can be part of that. You can be a trim tab too. All you have to do is join Planet Entrepreneur.

■ ■ ■

 The senior *USA Today* small business columnist and top-selling author, **Steve Strauss**, is also a spokesperson for corporations wishing to tap the small business marketplace, a recovering lawyer, and a frequent media guest on TV and radio. He sits on the advisory board of the World Entrepreneurship Forum and regularly speaks across the globe about entrepreneurial business strategies and global trends in business.

Steve's company, The Strauss Group, creates cutting-edge business content for everyone from Fortune 100 companies to the *Huffington Post*, small chambers of commerce, and many others. His latest venture is the tech start-up TheSelfEmployed.com.

You can reach Steve at sstrauss@mrallbiz.com.

INDEX